She

blinked:

THE BOOK OF ME

LAURINDA ANDUJAR

She blinked:

THE BOOK OF ME
LAURINDA ANDUJAR

T&J PUBLISHERS

A SMALL INDEPENDENT PUBLISHER WITH A BIG VOICE

Printed in the United States of America by
T&J Publishers (Atlanta, GA.)
www.TandJPublishers.com

All definitions used are from Dictionary.reference.com.

Cover design by Fluker (flukerdesignsandevents)
Photography by Kim Calhoun
Book format and layout by Timothy Flemming, Jr. (T&J Publishers)
Edits by The Invested Freedom Writer

ISBN: 978-1-7324905-3-6

To contact author, go to:

www.SheBlinked.com
www.HealTheCityInc.org
sheblinked314@gmail.com
Instagram: heal_the_city_inc.
Facebook: Laurinda Andujar

Dedications

This book is dedicated to the broken, the orphaned and the unloved. May you find peace and joy in the beauty that is in you.

I would like to thank my beautiful mother Rose Williams. Mom, you are undoubtedly the strongest woman I know. You sacrificed so much so that I could have life. You didn't look to the left or the right, you stayed focused on us the best way you could. You gave us the gift of tough love and we needed that.

To my little twin disasters, Terrence and Tanetra, you both have grown to be amazing mothers and fathers to my nephews and grandnieces. You are the epitome of the phrase "Love All Over." You both stood in the gap for me when I couldn't stand for myself.

To my Dad Wesley Jonathan Williams, thank you for serving your purpose in my life. I pray that God will heal you in the broken places. You deserve some happiness.

To my big brother Joe. I love you and I thank you for your protection. To My handsome intelligent sons Dominick, Donte and Julian, thank you for loving me when I was unlovable. I didn't do everything right, yet, you still loved me. Just feeling your touch at times kept me from jumping off a cliff. To Aneese, mommy will see you one day in heaven.

To Robin Sanders, sis you blessed me more than you could ever have imagined. The way you live your life is a true example for many. You stood in the gap for so many, not wanting a thing in return. You prayed for me when I couldn't speak, and you always corrected me in love.

To the Dr. Cassandra Parks, and Dr. Venice Daley, queens you pushed me to the brink and pulled me back to life. You saw in me what I didn't see in myself. You saw transformational leadership and you believed in me until I believed in myself.

To my beautiful Aunt Barbara Gainey, and the entire tribe, thank you for your love and leadership. You also loved me into submission and you wouldn't allow me to quit on my destiny. We are all Jackson strong. Madea and Mack Dixon, I will see you again.

To all the angels that I entertained unawares, thank you for sharing your light with me, even when I didn't know that I needed it. To God, my Father, my bestie and my Creator, Your ways are not like our ways, and Your thoughts are not like our thoughts. Thank you for making me in your image. I bless you for this heart of mine. May it continue to break for what breaks yours!

"We delight in the beauty of the butterfly, but rarely admit the changes it has gone through to achieve that beauty."
—*Maya Angelou*

Table of Contents

Preface

This book is based on my life, my experiences, my challenges, and my victories. My purpose for writing this book is to reveal and bring forth awareness to break the generational curses that have held us hostage for far too long.

This book challenges individuals and leadership at all levels, to look inward, examine, and address the issues that we have swept under the rug. The unspoken wrongs, that happened in our homes in the past, can no longer dwell there.

We only operate at full capacity when we walk in true authenticity. We have to embrace being naked before God and man if we expect to experience true healing. This book is for every woman, man, boy and girl who has ever experienced anything other than joy, unspeakable joy.

This book is empowering, inspiring and transformational. This book is designed to help every individual realize that they have potential, understanding that they can achieve anything, when they shift their mindset to see the positive in every challenging situation.

She Blinked

She (Shē): used to refer to a woman, girl, or female animal previously mentioned or easily identified

Blink (blingk): to open and close the eye, especially involuntarily; wink rapidly and repeatedly

N THE TWINKLING OF AN EYE, A SUDDEN SPARK, TWO forces become one, she blinked. The sound of murmurs, muffled sounds warmth and water all around. She was safe, but in an instant that would all change. *She Blinked.*

She didn't know why she was chosen. She didn't know what life had in store for her. All she knew was that through the birth canal, she arrived. She would always be looked at as being different; she would always be the odd girl out. She would have dreams, wild-life shattering dreams. She would be the center of everyone's attention, yet none would notice her. She could do no right, and she could do no wrong. *She blinked.*

Life would take twists and turns. She would cry one moment, and then in a split second be filled with laughter. She would be called brilliant, and in the same breath would be deemed certifiably crazy. *She blinked.*

No matter where she stood, she stood out. People loved her and hated her at the same time and couldn't explain why. *She blinked.*

She was born Laurinda Andujar, but her close friends called her Lala. She had two loving parents. Rose Mary and Wesley. Rose had not been served life on a golden platter and Wesley was the bad boy that played the good guy. Two forces would procreate and set into motion the next series of events that would forever shape Lala's life.

Lala's childhood would be plagued with flickers of memory bouncing on and off. More often than not, swiss-cheese, hole-riddled emotions would cause some memories to fade forever and some to flicker like the beams of neon sign that read "Vacancy".

They say when you have faced certain childhood traumas you tend to create an alternate reality. Fact becomes fiction and fiction; well it is the perception of reality. Lala would do and say things that she would never remember. She would make life up as she went on.

One of her very first memories would be of her preschool years. Back in the day they called it Head Start.

Head Start was a program for low-income families that gave children a chance at a brighter future. It was graduation day, she would wear her little cap and gown and she would get passed over for a snack. She would begin to cry and no one would notice her tears. What she thought was the end of the world, would only be the beginning of a lifetime of pain and suffering; unjustified pain and suffering and she would blink.

Maybe her tears were the first cry for help. Maybe her tears were a sign of her lashing out at humanity for being anything but humane to her. She would recall weeks before how she got scolded for telling her teacher that her grandmother had died. She just wanted some attention. She just wanted to be noticed. And she was noticed.

Why in the world would a child that small make up something like that? Was she wishing she was dead? Was that her way of burying a piece of herself? What could cause her at such a young age to say such things? It was the beginning of her other reality!

She would be awakened at odd hours of the night by soft touches. At first, it hurt and she would block out the pain and fade into her dark place. She would blink and she would be on another plain. She would be floating high in the sky, playing with the angels that were watching over her, but got so busy and forgot they were there to protect her.

The visits would become so frequent she began to lose herself. She would blink and she would be just a shadow. A shadow that was hurting. A shadow that was lost. A shadow of herself. A shadow that would take the form of whoever crossed her path.

The visitor would be someone she trusted. Someone who loved her. Someone that would warp her true sense of what love was. A generational curse that would claim yet another unsuspecting victim. Her tiny body would endure so much pain in the form of "I love you," and occasional you know it feels good. She would blink and she would be much older now and her body would begin to form. She looked at life through lenses of feigned ignorance.

She believed everything and trusted no one. She was the perfect oxymoron. She blinked, and she would have these thoughts. She would not know where they came from and it would scare her. Fear became her make-up, the very foundation of her being. It was the one thing she consistently applied daily.

Who could she talk to? No one would understand. They would blame her. Lala believed she was born with a Jezebel spirit, and it was somehow her fault. It had to be. She almost slipped and told someone, and was quickly reminded of the shame and embarrassment awaiting her. Life would not allow her to tell any one of her pain. She would walk through life with blinders on, wearing a mask. She would question herself. Self was a stranger to her. A cruel, uncaring stranger that would beckon her to hide in the shadows. Lala feared she would be found out. Tainted and unloved, there would be no hope. There would be no peace. There would be no way out. Simply put, she would be stuck.

The events in Lala's life would manifest in a whirlwind of words. These words would be manifested in patterns and rhythms that would sometimes soothe the savage beast within. More times often than not, those words would be spewed in a fury of unbridled anger and hurt. She would silently write. Life was the canvas that painted her unworthy. Unworthy of love, unworthy of happiness, unworthy of success. She may as well have been stillborn. And in some ways she was. She would walk through life motionless.

Each day would bring new questions, new mysteries, new issues, and hurts. She would tire of the newness. She would find herself longing for old faithful, old safety, old answers to why her questions continually went unanswered. Was she the only one enduring so much pain? Did God forget her? Did she do something somehow to lose His favor? *She blinked.*

What were these demons that Lala would speak of? They came in many forms: suicide, molestation, insecurity, self-hatred. Mimic….mimic, imitation of life. She would get so lost in the fantasy of life itself. She would live the lives of others and be content. She would start things and not finish. She couldn't finish, only whole things are finished. She was incomplete. She wasn't even real.

She lived in the shadows of others. Her song was made up of the notes of passersby. She would be pitied.

She did not know why she was being pitied. Nonetheless, she would be pitied, and she would love it, because it was attention, and she would unknowingly begin to do things to get attention. She would say things to get attention. And therefore, her body would get attention instead. She really didn't want to get that kind of attention. That was all she knew attention. She would shrink and all would be right with the world until he came. And he would again and again, rendering himself until almost nothing remained.

Didn't he know what he was doing to her? Didn't they know they were setting her up for failure? Wait, what... they? Yes, from an early age they would come and they would set her up for failure and she would go along for the ride, and she would know no better. And he, he would not protect her. It could have been worse. Wait, it was worse. She would wake up from nightmares that would turn into fright-mares. Remnants of touches and kisses that would claim another innocent victim. She didn't deserve this, but she didn't know any better. To her, it was normal. And he would come time and time again. He came in a different shade, shape or form, but he would come. And it would hurt.

Death would attempt to take her at a young age. Death came in a different shade, shape or form. Her beautiful big brown eyes were dead. They were dark; she was the picture of a perfect little angel. Yet, she experienced too much hurt to be innocent, experienced too much brokenness to remain whole. She was the one puzzle with all of the pieces that could not be put together.

Lala would blink and she would be walking to the store. The corner store was right across the street from the green wooden house. The perfect little green house that looked like love from the outside. It looked like love. The warmth felt like regret, death, disaster, and mayhem. It was her home. She would cross the gray paved two lane road to gather a glimpse of childhood and would end up only to narrowly escape yet another attempt on her innocence. He would whisper to get her attention. He would woo her, and try to coax her into a relaxed state. The big bad wolf had come and little brown riding hood would be sharp enough, have wisdom enough to recognize his call.

This time it would be different. His eyes were empty and she recognized the tricks. God would be watching over her, and He would allow her to remember something that she learned perhaps at school. NEVER TALK TO STRANGERS. She didn't remember what she went to the store for. She could only remember vividly, to this day, that little bare wooden shack standing in her path between that little green house and that corner store where it could have easily ended, but it didn't. Perhaps that is why to this very day she gets extremely bothered when she sees a young child walking alone.

Lala, the little girl with little promise, would live to die another day. She would sprint home to tell her daddy that a man had tried to get her to come into this place. She remembered that she told the man she would be back and to wait right there. She came back with her daddy and he would confront him. He would confront the big bad wolf and all would be right with the world. She would be safe from outsiders. Only, it did not go exactly as little brown envisioned it. To her surprise, they would indeed talk. They would talk, they would sit and talk like friends on that bench in the front of that corner store, and she would be amazed because he did not protect her. He was another one of them. Different face, different shape, same darkness and she would blink.

Many times in life, the things that we face shape our future. If you are lost, those things may latch on to you and you will take on its form. Like someone with sight impairment you may search for things, or people to lift you up. Those things in the end may only end up dragging you down. There is a process that you will have to go through to get from point A to point B. In the beginning was God. And God made men, and men made her suffer.

Life would frequently throw her a bone. A brief flicker of light. A hope of normalcy, which in itself was a joke. In between the lines she would admire a mother that stood up against the blows of domestic violence. A mother that would love a man that had other lovers, a man that had an insatiable desire for little delicacies wrapped in small frames. And comically, she could not hate him. He had to pick it up somewhere. Did he suffer the same tragedies as a child? He had to. It was a learned behavior.

Truthfully, the only thing that Lala would learn

early on was that she was nothing. Life had carelessly crafted the master without the peace, and she would funnel through life with blinders on. She would not be able to see people as they were for the masks they wore were beautiful. The masks they wore were inviting. The masks they wore were not her face starring back at her in the mirror riddled with guilt.

It would not matter how many layers Lala would put on, or take off for that matter. She would never be enough. She would never have enough. She would blink and she would find herself shedding everything she was or could ever hope to be, all for the sake of approval. Lala developed a knack for putting on heirs or skin that was as fragile as that of a cracked egg membrane to get by. The problem with getting by is that you never really get by.

The hand me down skin that she would wear far too often would be tattered. It would be ragged and it would reek of failure. The material would ultimately shed as poor fabric eventually does, and she would be left naked to the harsh winds of the world and she would blink.

> **Family** (fam-uh-lee, fam-lee): a basic social unit consisting of parents and their children, considered as a group, whether dwelling together or not:

She had a family, that beautiful green little house held her

21

family. That beautiful green little house held many secrets. That beautiful little green house betrayed her, and her family traditionally was anything but traditional.

Rose was a small framed woman that worked very hard for her family. She cared for her children and she vowed to keep her children safe. She vowed, she tried, and safety: it eluded her. *She blinked.*

One moment, Lala would be laying on her back on the floor of that beautiful little green house with her legs crossed half Indian style smiling and giggling up at the ceiling. The next moment, she would be awakened by screams. Horrible screams, earth shattering screams, there would be broken pane from the front door, and the happy memories would fade. *She blinked.*

Wesley would have returned home against the orders of the Clearwater police to claim his family. Only he really didn't want his family. He wanted to instill fear into Rose. He didn't want her to be happy, but wanted to be happy, and to be happy with others, and there were others. He could have populated the earth with his others, and that he did try.

If you are anything like me, you are probably wondering what in the world could possibly have been wrong with Rose? Heck, if I were on the outside looking in, I might have pondered the same. What forced her to stay? Did she have low self-esteem? Why hadn't she been enough? Was she enough? Enough of what? Don't get me wrong, Rose was more than enough. She was beautiful, caring, kind, and trusting. She loved Wesley more than life itself and he knew it. He was so sure of it that on numerous occasions he would attempt to take life itself from her. He would draw on her life like a pin-less ATM machine with no limit and no replenishment. He took advantage of her. He would charm her, then he would beat her. He would coax her, then he would kick her. He would woo her, and he would win. He would win, and Lala, she would lose.

Fade to black and Lala would be sitting at the dinner table enjoying a seafood feast that her mom Rose prepared after a long hard day's work. Wesley would be missing in action, most likely out somewhere defending his manhood. She would be laughing at her little twin siblings and her mom singing to them as they watched fantasy island.

She remembered that island vividly, as she would often visit there to escape life. Her beautiful green little house was a happy house until… she blinked. He would be coming through the front door with a gun or a steel pipe in his hands. He intended to break the silence of happiness. Rose would not have time to collect her three little brown valuables. She would barely have time to collect herself, and so naked she ran into the night; a flight for life. Lala would awaken to a still house. Her little twin siblings would be fast asleep with no inkling of the pain and suffering that Rose would face with each blink. Lala would wait in concern for her mother to return and she would not blink. Lala would not move. She couldn't move. Couldn't breathe, couldn't see. She would be paralyzed to everything but fear and the pounding of her non-existent heart. She longed to blink; blink to the next chapter, blink to safety. Blink to something except the loneliness that began to consume her.

One would wonder if there were going to be any consequences for his actions. He seemed to destroy everything he touched, and he was untouchable. At that moment in time Wesley's reach was like the hand of God. Instead of displaying what true authentic love looked like, he would warp Lala's view of love. And she would look for that warped sense of love in every relationship moving forward.

Excuse me for the leap frog through time. This roller coaster of emotions was exactly what I felt every second, every minute of each and every day. It is most likely the reason for the gaping holes that exist in her pockets of memories. It had been a wonder that there had not been more suicide attempts, more mental breakdowns, and more knock down, drag out fights with self...and she would blink.

Rose was safe; she was barely alive, but she was alive. It is amazing what the will to live will do for an individual. Lala would never know what was going through the mind of her mother in those moments, she would only be grateful that Juliana chose life.

Lala would blink and she herself would be jumping from her bedroom window. She would be screaming out into the night for help and she would have a flash back to Rose. Twenty something and wondering how in the world did I end up repeating the past. She would scream once more and be taken in by a neighbor who heard the faint screams muffled by two large hands caressing her throat with great force, and she would blink.

Consequence

Love by consequence
Not like that
Love by incident
Incidentally do you love me?
If I say it
Why can't you say it to me?
Lala
You ain't got nothing to say
What's going on fam
Back to one
Lala
Do you hear me?
I love you
Peace
Place that in your memory
Guilt trips
Smooth as bullshit from your lips
Aimed at me
Keep talking
I'm glad that's what you think about me

That calm line I was walking
Just got bumpy
Heart skipped a beat
Beauty beneath
Swept deep
A second more
Screams
What you don't conquer you're destined to repeat
Tied up in bloody sheets
The pounding of heavy feet
As you jump of a window
Determined to greet the
Face of a new day
To black you fade
As you feel the heat of your breath
In the air
The blank stares of the grim reaper
Praying your seed is safe from the creeper
You found yourself in a relationship with
Someone please press fast forward
And skip this storyline
I never imagined this
Would be mine
My life playing out

Flash back to Rose. Rose would soon reveal that after pounding door to door that any elderly couple would provide shelter from the grim reaper. The grim reaper was handsome. The grim reaper wore a smile that could light up the darkest night. The grim reaper could coax the wax off a candle and the grim reaper went by the alias of Wesley.

Even though Juliana would survive she would not escape the consequences of Wesley's love. She would be hospitalized and suffer from internal bleeding and she would no longer be able to bare children ever again. Wesley had kicked her in her stomach so hard that she had to have an emergency hysterectomy. She would be swollen, she would be broken up, but by grace she would be alive and she would blink.

Left in pieces would be the only way that Lala would know how to exist. To fit in with this group she would be kind, to fit into this group she would be quiet, to fit in with another group she would be hood. She would know Christ somewhere in there, but she would never know relationship with any group. She was the missing link that no one knew was missing and she would blink.

Questioning her very existence would consume her. She longed to fit in. She longed to relate, she wanted to be relate-able. She was the caterpillar entangled in an iron clad cocoon that refused to release her. She wasn't beauty. She wasn't love. She was rejection. She was hatred. She didn't have two thoughts to rub together of her own and her soul was bone dry. She lived in the valley of the dry bones awaiting a savior.

Be Here

I didn't ask to be here
But I am
I didn't ask for your love
But I can
And that got me no where
Canned emotions
With a sprinkle of this
A sprinkle of that
Every trained magician
Pulling tricks out of their hats
A series of illusions
Made specifically for me
Tricks that mask my beauty
In shadows of hurt
DNA infused with dirt
Hues of brown
Settling down
Confused by its makeup
Get me out of this nightmare
I can't wake up
Better yet sandman
Dust me back to sleep
My dreams are an altered reality of me
I've lost control
My soul isn't that deep
My emotions have control
I've sprung a leak
I am drowning

The blank spots in her memory, and the gaping holes in her life would be a security blanket that she could not afford to outgrow. Those holes would also be the only way that she would have a false sense of wholeness, and the ability to connect the dots to the universe that held her. Her universe would provide rainy days to camouflage the tears that frequently flowed. Perhaps that would be the reason that she longed for the rainy days.

Blank Spots

I have blank spots in my memory
Blurry vision and polka dots hinder me
From seeing the entrance
That obstructs the hallway
To my destiny
This house has no doors
No windows to escape this pain
I hear the muffled sounds of rain
The pitter patter rhythm is driving me insane
I feel the cool of the breeze
The steps of others beneath my feet
Attempting to guide me
To the gust of fresh wind that lifts me
Instantly I am let down
Clouds taunt me
With the cleansing ability
Of fresh rain

Precipitation
My brain blocks me
All these voices in my head
Screams
I mean
I wish
I could dream
Bridge the gap to the scene
That was torn from my memory
Then maybe I would be whole

Others would see her gloom and blame it on the rain. She was not aware of how to own her atmosphere that would allow her to frame her thinking. If only she could frame her thinking, she could change her life, and change her situation. Her current situation would lend to fears; that would lend to tears; that would lend to hurt; that would lend to many days of contemplated suicide; many attempts and many failures. Thank God for the failure! *She blinked.*

Holding, she stood there like a plane awaiting take off. All systems were a go. There was no traffic buildup. The skies were clear, there was complete and utter silence in the control tower, no movement, nothing but silence and there she stood… *She blinked.*

Eventually, Rose would muster the strength to move on with her life she would settle for Mr. Right Now. She wasn't interested in being controlled, manipulated, or used. She had found a facsimile of strength. It was as true to the copy of strength she could afford. She would pick up the broken shards of her soul, and do the best she could to emulate life as it should be for her precious jewels.

Days would be hard, but she would make it. Ends would barely meet, but she would make it. Long nights, longer nightmares, silent screams, emotional distress, but she would make it...and she would blink.

Rose weighed the options for herself and for her children. She would end up concluding that she must get out of Clearwater to provide a better life for her children. Lala would blink and her mother would be gone.

She never questioned if her mother loved her. She knew she did, but yet again she would blink and she would be lonely. Her mother would leave her and her siblings in the care of a close family friend by the name of Donna. Donna was as sweet as pie could be, she cared for Rose and the twins like they were her own.

Lala, for the first time in her life, would feel a sense of normalcy. She would be in an environment that was conducive to family and growth. Well, you know the funny thing about growth is that growth can be gradual in its stages or there can be a spurt that happened all of the sudden, and sometimes growth can be painful. And we all know tumors and cancers are referred to as growths.

And there was a cancer that Lala would be left to deal with on her own, his name would be Mr. Right Now. He was Rose's former Mr. Right Now and he tried to steal

Lala's joy. Lala would blink, and she would recall the night Mr. Right Now would be left alone while Rose was at work providing for her family and Mr. Right now, would call Lala into the bathroom and she would come, unsuspecting she would come; because surely the big bad wolf with all his huffing and puffing would never make it into the three little pigs home, but then again, her little green house was made of wood.

When Lala reached the bathroom, Mr. Right would be sitting naked as the day he was born in a tub of water and he would place her tiny hand on his privates. Lala would feel violated, and she hated him. In a cowardly fashion, he would threaten to kill her if she told anyone, and she would add another secret to her fright-mare bank, and it would collect interest. *She blinked.*

See, Mr. Right was Donna's brother and Lala would cower in secret as Rose went off to make a better life for her family. Lala soon discovered that divine intervention would be her destiny in this story. She would somehow muster up the strength to tell what happened between her and Mr. Right and she would be awakened by the Clear-water police. They had come to save her. They had come to take her away to safety. *She blinked.*

Leaning Stick

I am tired of standing

I see a shadow that's lending
Me a helping hand
This crutch
I lust for to ease my pain
Sends signals to my brain
A sign of hope
A feeling of euphoria
To help me cope
In my time of need
I breathe as they grip around my chest
Chokes me at best
Cardiopulmonary resuscitation
Is my destination
To live at best
To survive
Scratch that
My will to thrive
Just kicked in
Looks like I am going to win
Redemption from sin
Is closer than I think
She blinked

Wesley had gotten word that Rose was out of pocket. He would come once again to claim his family. He would come not because he missed his children, but to hurt Rose once more. And there was nothing she could do about it, because... *she blinked.*

For the first time in her life, Lala would not be

scared. She would be scarred but no longer scared. She would get her first taste of victory by standing up to the big bad wolf and she would in. She was out of his reach and away from his touch. This win, only being temporary, was a win nonetheless.

Lala would be free from the little green house only to trade it in for a bigger version of the little green house, and a large version of that little brown shack. Blink forward. She is now nested in a small town, where everybody knows your name, everybody goes to church on Sunday, and everyone looked out for each other.

Lala and her siblings had become the foster kids of freedom. She would never believe that her life would become the sum of fragmented visits of others. She would be introduced to the others that would assume the role of Aunt, Uncles, Cousins, and others and they would mold her and help to mend her. The makers hands were working, and she would not realize that this was all part of the process to repair her brokenness.

Lala would be agitated by love, then tossed by turmoil. She would be afflicted and then shown affection. She would be taught to stand only to have the ground ripped from under her feet, but she was now planted firm, and she would grow. This was the beginning of her seasoning. She would meet her Great Grandmother and Grandfather, they would introduce her to God.

Madea would teach Lala how to be gentle and kind. She was a short woman with warm brown eyes and an enormous heart. Madea was known for taking children and the unwanted into her arms and introducing them to love. She understood that everyone served a purpose and deserved to feel loved, if nothing else. She was the epitome of the old school mother, and mother she did.

She would nurture Lala so much, up until this day, no one would be able to convince Lala that she wasn't blood. In fact, she was better that blood. She held the super power of keeping the wolves at bay … if only for a short while.

Madea was only about 5'2 but she stood as tall as a 7 foot man. She had a strength about her that could tear down hatred with a bow of the head. She was a mother of the community. She was a pillar of the community and she was afraid of nothing.

Madea loved without limits, and her love knew no bounds. She truly ruled the roost and Mack allowed her to. He had no choice. Lala would blink and Madea would be sitting in her pew at church with her knocking stick. She would beat that stick to the rhythm of the hymns that would be pounded out to the drums and like life she would never miss a beat. Lala couldn't recall ever really hearing her speak as she sat in those pews. What she would notice was her strength, and the steady rhythm that beat like a heart as it hit the wooden floor of that little white church.

With every strike of the stick Lala could feel the clock of her life ticking. The longing for spirituality growing in her. The will to live rising up and she would be confident if only for a moment, in the presence of Madea. Lala would blink, and she would be standing over Madea's coffin, and she would cry. She would not only cry, she would throw herself across Madea's body and she would weep for all of humanity.

Humanity took such a blow the day that God recovered an angel called Madea. Madea was the first real idea of what life was to be like. The first glimpse of hope and impact. Lala loved Madea. She would blink and she would recover Madea in the smoke of her memories for years to come, and as usual, Madea would release kisses of strength to Lala in gusts of wind. And she would remember Madea and she would smile.

Madea, affectionately known as Mother Dear

Beauty to the nth degree
Danger would never stand around me
When you were near
Fear was never an issue for me
You allowed me to see clearly
Dearly your loved me
You were my Mother Dear
The finest pedigree
You were
Introduced the stars to me
Told me that I was far from the being

INTRODUCTION: SHE BLINKED

That earth told me to be
You crafted me purity
Protected me form the rejection button
That others pressed play for me
Held my face in your hands
When men struck at me
Nightly you prayed for me
When others neglected me
Broke the spirit of incest from me
Kept me when the wolf tested me
You should me I was a jewel
Too rare to see
The flaws in me as nothing less that beauty
You molded me
Took control of me
When my mind hindered me
From living
Giving all that was inside of me
A chance to break free of the curses
That lurked around me
Quietly tapping out the beat
On your tapping stick of love
Placing me on your family tree
beloved

Madea was married to Dixon. Dixon was a tall slender handsome man. He, like Madea, was well respected in the community. He was a business man that worked very hard for his family. He cared for Madea and gave her the world.

He was the first positive role model that Lala would encounter. His motives were clear. He held no secrets, and he was the first true demonstration to Lala, as to what the head of the household should look like.

He would never be judgmental. He would never raise his voice or his hand, and he would protect his family to the end. He was the founder of that little white church with endless possibilities. He built that church by hand. His sweat, tears, and love went into that church. Every Sunday and mid-week service he would pour out love into others.

Lala would blink, and Dixon would be much older and his frame would be slightly bent. She would recall one of the few statements of this tall mighty warrior; God is watching you. These four simple words that would impact Lala the rest of her life and she would blink...and he would be gone.

Dixon would be gone and she would miss him. She could do nothing to bring him back. She would hold onto the memories that would forever linger in her mind. She would see him as the perfect man that would never manifest again into her life...and she would blink.

Strength

Strong tower
Power in the way that your voice rises and falls

INTRODUCTION: SHE BLINKED

Standing behind the pulpit
Or building a fence
To keep the animals at bay
Your way of dealing with life
Intrigues me
Empowers me to be
At one with the me
The creator intended me to be
You are the perfect man
That never existed
When pain came
You kissed it goodbye
Scriptures you read to me
Prayers you prayed for me
Somehow you knew what I was up against
In an instant
You covered me
You reminded me
That I was beauty
You fulfilled the duty
Of fatherhood
Father good
You were to me
And my siblings
Wiped off the dribbling
Of tears that smeared my face
With hate
Self-loathing
You clothed me
In love
Kisses that I missed
That reminded me

What childhood should be
A net of safety

For years to come, bitter would be intertwined with the sweet. Flickers of hope and hopelessness would create cavities in her mind, and she would wander through life. She would stumble, sometimes fall, sometimes get up, and sometimes choose to wallow like a swine in filth, and she would not blink. She would develop blank spots to shield her from the worries of the world. She would rise to the occasion only to flop to failure. She would have failed relationships. She would Mimic... mimic.. mimic that imitation of life. Her brain would go offline to escape the virus that was life, and she would reboot to try to face another day.

Life, like the lights would blink on and off, and a glimpse of hope could be seen far off in the distance and she would smile. She loved that little town because that little town brought her joy. She had a family that loved on her. She would be fed spiritually, emotionally and physically. The small little town that held her began to nourish her soul, even with the big bad wolf being only a stone's throw away.

On Sundays, she would go to Sunday school and church, then muddle through the week, and then be replenished by mid week service. They say a week with out God makes one weak. She surely could feel the strength being etched into her very fabric. She found her voice and oh could she sing. She felt unstoppable! Whenever she was standing before the congregation she was at peace.

She would learn that she possessed the ability to make people smile. She possessed the ability to make people forget their problems, and she could be in the spot light. Maybe those moments that fed her need for attention would be the reason she would blink and later in life would find herself needing to please others. For now, her voice was beautiful, and her voice would negate the fact that she was tattered and torn.

For once in her life, her notes would not fall on deaf ears. She could cry and rejoice. She could hide her pain in praise. She would develop a praise that she and God could only understand. She would blink, and she would be reminded that God does not operate in secrets. However, in secrets was the only way she knew to survive. And in secrets she stayed.

Secrets

I live in the land of secrets
Where men do not know my tales
They do not hear my cries
Or notice the pain in my eyes
They do not attempt to pay a fair wage
When they thrust me on center stage

Puppet by day
Puppet by night
I can't free myself from your handle
No matter how hard I try
I try to escape this thorn in my side
A gaping hole in my soul
And I scream only to wake
Up in this dream
That shall never be told
These dreams seem reoccurring
And yes they are quite disturbing
You only notice the smile on my face
Which isn't a smile at all
You attempt to pick me up
When I'm standing up
And push me down when I fall
I dwell in the land of secrets
And that is where I'll stay
Here no one knows I'm hurting
I sit and await daybreak
I dwell in the land of secrets
My secrets are unnerving

She would blink, and someone would discover that she was talented, her life would change forever, and she would be a star. She imagined one day that she would be on stage and everyone would be calling her name. They would admire her gorgeous voice and her beautiful face; that flawless skin. Microphone in hand and the spotlight on her, the chanting, smiling, laughter, but the laughter was at her expense. She would not be called beautiful, she would not be the envy of every man, but she would be talented and she would get noticed, and her voice would get her one step closer to fame, if only for an instant.

Lala's habit of not following through would cost her a chance of a lifetime that she would never forget. She was almost famous. The Jezebel spirit had once again overcome this shy, quiet girl one night at a concert in that little small town. It was the music, the music made her come alive, it made her dance. She would have no control over her body, and the rhythmic tones beckoned her. The music pulled her body to and fro, and her body swayed and liked it. All eyes would be on her. Some in utter disbelief that a young body could move like that. Some appalled at the sinner that stood before them, and some, no doubt, in awe of the way her body flitted on the notes that hung above their heads, and danced between their ears, and rest assured, the wolf pack were at attention. When all was said and done, despite the doubters, she was still noticed for her voice.

Lala Gazelle 2.27.13

She is the defender of man reborn
She has the upper hand in the eye of a storm
She is more that she could ever imagine to be

She is made by God perfectly
She has flaws, yet she is whole
Her core is warm in the center of the cold
Filled earth her birth by baptism
In a world filled by cynicism

Girl Time 3.3.13

It was her time
Since inception
Life would take its toll
And the joker card
Deception
Would leave her bound
Peace she thought
For her
Would not be found
She would love hard
And it would not be returned
She would give of herself
And the passion she yearned
Would return to her void
She would get lost in the noise
Of let downs and no's
Inhumanity would toss her back
To and fro
Whenever she gave
It was never enough
The pain she endured
Coined her short of breathe

INTRODUCTION: SHE BLINKED

In constants she wept
Constant hurt
Constant rain
Constant insecurities
Disdain
Self loathing
Her pain
Lead her to live in shadows of self
If only the mirror
Would reveal her wealth
She was the mother of beauty
The mother of life
The was the mother of joy
On the road to strife
She was the sign of redemption
The face of grace
She was the victory
That didn't comprehend
She had already won the race
She was the one that kept on gifting
Until she had nothing left to give
She was the one that didn't
Understand her purpose
The reason that God birthed her
Until she cried out in the name of Jesus
What she found
Was her will to live
She heard the voice of God
Say Live
Thrive
You will not just survive
I give you life

That you may live it more abundantly
If you would just
Trust in me
She found her music
She found her choice
She found her beauty
She found her voice
There was a reason to live
A reason to love
A reason to celebrate life
She was daughter of Zion
Royalty ran through her blood
She was the daughter of glory
She was the sister of grace
She was the very likeness of His face
She was the epitome of peace
She learned to walk by Faith

CHAPTER 1

Fantasy Island

Fan·ta·sy (fan(t)esē): the faculty or activity of imagining things, especially things that are impossible or improbable ("his research had moved into the realm of fantasy").

THEY SAY WHEN WE FACE SPECIFIC CHILDHOOD traumas we tend to create alternate realities. Facts are no longer relevant nor welcomed, and fiction becomes the new truth, a new means of escape. That was the case concerning me. There was a big difference between the world I lived in and the world I often fantasized about living in at night.

My childhood is peppered with good and bad memories. Among my fondest memories is one of my two younger siblings and I sitting at the dinner table in our little green wooden house in Clearwater, Florida. I was the oldest of three. My mom had just finished cooking the most fantastic dinner. She said we could have anything we wanted—it was payday! She had prepared a seafood feast worthy of King Triton himself, and she was smiling while standing over us. She was wearing a pair of brown velor jogging shorts with a solid white stripe down the sides, a yellow top, and a navy blue doo rag. She wore these stylish large framed 70's style brown tinted glasses.

Even though she was only 5'3, she had legs for days. She was beauty, brains, and strength neatly woven together. She catered to me, and my little twin brother and sister like we were royalty. In the back of my mind, I always wondered why my mom was so giving and so loving. Was it because she wanted the best for us? Undoubtedly, she inherited those traits from her mother, my grandmother. Surely. The thing that stood out the most to me was her beautiful smile. I loved that smile!

Momma was a cheerleader in high school, which explains her bubbly personality. She was always kind and soft-hearted. She hardly raised her voice at anyone. She was always doing things to please others. As some would say, she never met a stranger. While mom was in high school, she dated a football player named Jerry, which apparently didn't end well for her. That relationship left her with invisible scars that have haunted her even to this day. Whatever happened between the two of them was pushed aside as they agreed to move on with their lives. But mom never really moved on mentally. The pain of what happened was too intense.

Mom went on to graduate from high school with a 4.0-grade point average, and Jerry went off to college with no worries. For mom, the transition from high school to adult life wasn't as smooth. She had gotten pregnant. She was only 18 years old at the time. It's difficult enough being single with a child these days, so you could imagine how tough it was for a single teenage mother back then. She endured much criticism, and was shunned because of her decision to bring a child into this world. People would say, "She's just a baby having a baby." But mom didn't care though. She decided to keep her baby and named him Joey.

It just so happened that Joey didn't live with us, even though we were only two years apart. I didn't learn much about him until I was older. My mom didn't talk about him, so we never asked. There was a reason for him not being with us, which only she knew. Whatever the reason was, it must have been hard for her.

My brother and sister were twins. They were four years younger than me, and at the time I really didn't like them. Don't get all judgmental on me. It was hard being the only child and then someone else comes along and steals your spotlight. That was a tough adjustment for me. And…let's just say, things happened. I'm often reminded of the time I cut off of my little sister's hair right before Easter when my mom wasn't looking.

Conveniently, I can't recall all of the specifics of

that incident, but every now and then my momma would ask me, "Do you remember that time I walked over to the store and you ran to the door saying, 'Look, momma! I did Tanetra's hair for you?!'" Up until this very day, momma reminds me of this. My sister, Tanetra, also reminds me of this before reassuring me that payback is coming. Of course, after that, we just laugh. A little sibling rivalry never hurt anyone. Well, in some cases it hasn't.

Holidays were a big deal to my mom. She would dress us in the frilliest, most girlie girl dresses she could find, and load our hair with so many barrettes we could hardly hold up our heads. Tanetra would only need one since she barely had any hair. The colors of the barrettes weren't even uninformed. It's like she just threw them on top of our heads, and where ever they landed is where they stayed. Bless her soul. My mom had two girls, but she couldn't do hair to save her life.

And poor Terrence, he would always have to wear these tight little three-piece suits that looked like they irritated his skin, and an afro that was taller than he was. He looked like a tiny Gary Coleman, just as adorable.

My mama loved family time. It was as if she lived for these moments. On nights like this one, mom would make sure our bellies were full and then we'd slip into our pajamas and get ready to watch our favorite television show together, Fantasy Island. The show would always start with the sound of the low hum of an airplane engine in the distance, and as it drew nearer, that's when the symphony started playing. The music would start off slow, and then pick up allowing everyone to hear the notes dancing. Then suddenly, there it was, Fantasy Island!

When Fantasy Island came on I couldn't wait for Tattoo (the small person) to run up the circular stairs of the Queen Anne Cottage to the white tower with red trimming, ring the large liberty like bell, and then scream down to Mr. Roarke (played by Ricardo Montalban), "De plane, boss!! De plane!!" Tattoo and Mr. Roarke would then open the windows to his island cottage, serve up a debonair smile and wait for the giggling island girls to run past him, then he would glide down the steps, get into the red and white striped tapestry covered jeep, and rush to meet the guests that were arriving on the island.

Before the guests would arrive, Mr. Roarke would straighten his black silk tie and make sure his off-white cotton suit and hair were perfect, then he would throw his hands up like that of a maestro and say in a thick Latin accent, "Smiles. Smiles, everyone." He was a very handsome man, standing six feet tall. To me, he looked like a giant compared to Tattoo who was only 3'10. He'd clap, signaling the musicians to play, and then the dancers would begin to sway, shake, and stir up excitement.

At the beginning of every episode, I couldn't wait to see who the special guest would be. They always had a star-studded line up on the show. Oh, how I wished that I was one of those characters. I had a few wishes I wanted the dream-maker on that island to grant me.

The guests would be greeted with a colorful cocktail of their choice after stepping off the plane, then Mr. Roarke would provide a sneak peek into the fantasies of the guests. He provides for us, the viewers, just enough to keep us on the edges of our seats waiting for more.

In one episode, Mr. Roarke took out his pocket watch and looked down at Tattoo and said, "Our guests are arriving on time, to the second," Tattoo responded,

"They always do, and you always act like it's a miracle!" Mr. Roark then exclaimed,

"My dear Tattoo, when each guest is paying 50,000 dollars for a three-day stay on Fantasy Island, he or she DESERVES a miracle!"

Whoa! You heard right, folks. $50.000! Now, mind you, this show aired in the 70's. Let me put this into perspective for you. During this time, a new house was $32,500, a brand-new car was only $3,950, gasoline was $.40 per gallon, you could buy essential food items such as sugar, milk, coffee, bacon, eggs, hamburgers, and bread for only $5, and the tuition cost at Harvard University was only $3,000 a year.

People were paying $50,000 for three days of miracles and fun. Unbelievable! That particular episode resonated with my soul. In that episode, there was a young lady who had been severely burned and scarred in a house fire when she was young, and both of her parents ended up dying. She had been shuffled around from foster home to foster home after that. She had a really tough life. She grew up poor, and with low self-esteem. And she was in and out of the prison system. She was angry with the world and plummeting towards destruction fast.

In a twist of fate, her parole officer took her to Fantasy Island, in the hope that she would finally learn to see past her scars, and recognize once more the beautiful young woman she was. The young woman was angry, rude, and devoid of hope. Mr. Roarke, however, had a way of making people see things differently. He gave the young woman a magic potion that took away her outward scars, but then he let her know that it would be up to her to make the inward scars go away. Truth be told, although outside scars may never go away, as I would soon discover, it's better to live with a scarred outer appearance than to live with a mutilated inner man.

In the end, that young woman found happiness even though her scars eventually reappeared; but she was finally able to see the value of her inner-self first, and she learned to accept and love who she was. That episode did it for me. What Mr. Roarke helped that young woman to discover in nearly 40 minutes is what it took me almost 40 years to learn.

That television show filled me with many beautiful fantasies. It took my mind on an imaginative trip. There were 152 episodes and 7 seasons of that show, and I watched them all. Each show had two storylines, and I would melt into each event as if I were on the screen. Every week, I couldn't wait to cozy up with my momma and my siblings and watch the always graceful Mr. Roarke and Tattoo make dreams come true.

Looking back, when I think about the cost of having your fantasies come true, $50,000 for a three-day excursion to Fantasy Island is a small price to pay for happiness, even if that happiness was only temporary.

As a little girl, I'd often wonder how my stay on the island would be. Would I be rich or a famous movie star? Would everybody love me? I pondered so much over Fantasy Island that it would cross over into my reality. I'd imitate the characters on the show, the guests namely, picturing myself in their shoes. I dreamed so much about Fantasy Island that the characters from that show overshadowed pockets of my memories.

I guess, wherever you are trouble will always find you if it's meant to. Herve Villechaize, the French-born actor of English and Filipino descent, who was known to the world as Tattoo, handcrafted thousands of fantasies for others during their stay on the island. He worked tirelessly to create precious moments for other people. He was catering to them while masking his own pain. Sadly, on September 5th of 1993, my beloved friend, Tattoo, which Herve played from 1977-1984, had succumb to bouts of depression and alcoholism and took his own life. There would be no more ringing of the bell by Tattoo. I would no longer hear "De plane! De plane!" There would be no more fantasies to turn into reality by him. There would only be the cruel, harsh reminder that money can't buy us an escape from the internal turmoil ravaging us from within.

Even though Tattoo and Mr. Roarke are no longer on that island, I still have a tendency of finding my way back there. I can't tell you how many hours I spent playing out in my head the fantasy life that escaped me at home. Perhaps, this is why I have such an intense longing to be near the water. This may be why I love sitting quietly on the beach so much. I sometimes feel as if I can get lost in the waves. I even longed at times to get lost at sea like the cast of another show I loved, Gilligan's Island.

Gilligan's Island was about a diverse group of people who chartered a small boat to go on a three-hour tour, only to be lost at sea. I know you are singing the theme song as you read this, so am I. These people ended up being castaways.

It was crazy how they had plenty of resources and opportunities to get off of that island, but they never left. It seemed crazy to me that they could make radios out of coconuts, and build satellites from bamboo sticks, but couldn't build a raft. The crew was always holding on to the past, desperately clinging to the memories of who or what they could have been. They were their own worst enemies, and their own saviors wrapped up in one. Theodore Roosevelt reminds us that "Comparison is the thief of joy." I spent many days and nights comparing myself to those around me, both on and off the screen while hoping to capture joy in a bottle.

I'd spend many days and nights wondering why I was born. I'd imagine that it was a grand event: A sudden spark emerged, and then two forces became one; the angels were taking their time while God carefully picked the two people that would care for me. Later through the years, I began to question why I was chosen, and if God had anything to do with my being here at all. Don't take this the wrong way, because I love my momma and I learned to love my daddy. While fantasizing about being on Fantasy Island, my reality wasn't a day at the beach. It was no picnic.

My mom did the best she could do while raising three kids and always having to look over her shoulder. She tried to give us the best. We went on Disney vacations. We always had a home cooked meal. I heard someone say that my mom could make a meal out of dishwater and a washrag—she was that resourceful. We always had Christmas presents under the tree. She made sure we were the best-dressed kids on the block, and she took us everywhere—and I do mean "everywhere." When she didn't have a car, she would pack us up and take us on an adventure on the city bus, even if we were only going to the grocery store. We were always with her. She'd take us walking, and when she did get blessed with a car, things got even better for us. She tried to make our reality mimic our dreams as much as possible.

I remember when mom took us on a ride in her car; it felt like we were on a roller coaster. We were driving down the street, and my little brother and sister were tucked safely in their seat-belts. Back then, I don't think car seats were a thing, and if they were, we couldn't afford them. I don't know what made me look up, but I did, and there, in a car besides ours, was my daddy. Daddy had another woman in the car with him. She was laughing and having a good time apparently. Momma got so angry at the sight of him and his other woman that she starting hitting his car with her car right there in the middle of the street. It looked like they were playing bumper cars. I believe that she would have killed him that day if she could. I was too young at the time to understand the pain of the type of betrayal mom experienced by my dad. I didn't understand why a man who made a vow to love, protect, and honor my mom in the sanctity of marriage was now sitting in a car adjacent to ours with another woman next to him. The concept of cheating, and infidelity, had not yet settled in my mind, but I'd later find out myself what that felt like.

I can't remember everything else that happened that night after momma encountered daddy on the road. A lot of things I'd block out of my mind. While mom was angry and teary-eyed, I was on Fantasy Island in my mind. While mom was stressing in the other room, I was on Fantasy Island. While mom was pacing the floor at night trying to figure out how she was going to make ends meet, I was on Fantasy Island. That's where I stayed. That's where I lived. That was my residence. When it was time to snuggle up together with my mom and siblings in front of the television to whisk away to that exotic island (Fantasy Island) for a new adventure, that was the happiest time on earth. I was in heaven. I was in a blissful paradise. The aura of a dream world fascinated me.

And then daddy came home. The fantasy was now over. My nightmare just stepped through the door.

Daddy's Home

I HAD A FAMILY THAT LIVED IN A LITTLE GREEN WOODEN house on Garden Avenue. That beautiful small, green house sat nestled quietly next to the street, and it held my family. And my beautiful little green home held secrets. That cute little green house betrayed me, and my family traditionally was anything but traditional.

One could get a false sense of security looking at our house from the outside. It seemed safe and cozy. I looked like it had love busting at the seams. That little green house is probably the reason why when I drive down the street, I question what goes on behind closed doors. I imagine evil in its unadulterated form.

My momma tries to forget that house, and she gets a glazed look to this day when you mention it. I wonder what happened there even before I was born. I guess I will never know. And for my momma's sake, I will never ask

59

again.

When I think of family I see moms being overly protective, kissing boo-boos, getting breakfast ready, and the kids going off to school. I had often longed for my momma to meet me at the school bus and have a snack waiting for me. There were times that she couldn't because my dad was too busy taking care of other women, so my mom had to pick up the slack.

If I could have asked for anything, anything in the world, I would have petitioned God to allow Janie and Mack to be my parents. Don't get me wrong, my mom was an amazing woman, but she couldn't protect us. She had a hard-enough time trying to protect herself from daddy. I guess I watched too many episodes of *Good Times*, *What's Happening*, and *The Cosby Show* and believed the hype that I could have it all.

I was blessed to have Janie and Mack Dixon in my life. Janie was a small framed woman, much like my mom. Janie was the picture of love. She was a church mother and a pastor's wife. She took care of all the abandoned, unloved children in the neighborhood. She often took care of the twins, my brother Joey, and me, not that we weren't loved. She took care of us because my mom would not be able to. It wasn't until I was in my late thirties did I learn that we were not actually blood relatives. Janie taught my mom how to cook, and how to be a wife, and she would do the same for me.

Now on to granddaddy Mack. My granddaddy

was a tall man. Very slender and handsome. He didn't say much, and a look was pretty much all it took. He was so tall that he had to duck under the door frame to walk inside of the house. I had a great deal of respect and love for my granddaddy. He was a real man's man, and he cherished my grandma.

She was Queen of his kingdom. I never saw him raise his voice nor his hand towards Janie. To me, they were the picture-perfect couple. They provided what I would say was normalcy for the first time in my life. At least that is the picture that my great grandparents painted for me. The view was perfect, and I felt normal. And normal was welcomed.

Granddaddy was a protector! I remember my Aunt telling the story of how back in the day in the City of Rosewood, a white woman accused a black man of raping her to hide the fact that she was having an affair. Well in racist fashion the lynch mob used that as an opportunity to kill as many blacks as their frustration would allow. My granddaddy sent my Grandma Janie along with her sisters to Gainesville to escape any impending danger.

When I finally got a chance to see the film, I couldn't help but imagine my granddaddy in action. And I was super proud. I even took a trip out to Rosewood and saw the house of the shop owner, as well as a portion of the train that was left there as a reminder of what happened. Nothing made me puff up more than when granddaddy started explaining to the boys how he would have "killed them men if he had to. My granddaddy was also a preacher. He not only walked the talk, he taught the talk. And I love him for that.

It's incredible that granddaddy was one of the few men in my life that did not sexually victimize me. In fact, he lifted me up. He protected me and never approached me threateningly. He was a hardworking man; a gentle giant of sorts. Man, I miss my granddaddy. It goes to show you that you don't have to be blood to be family. We will come back to Janie and Mack later.

When I hear the word daddy, I imagine seeing the wife and children rushing to the door screaming daddy's home. After a long day on the job, his family is just the breath of fresh air he needed. He may come bearing gifts for the kiddos, maybe a baby doll for myself and my sister, and a toy car or kite for my little brother. He was a hardworking man that always puts his family first, and he would be a protector. We never received any of those things.

I do believe there was a time that I really did love my daddy. My daddy was charming too. He could charm the stripes off a zebra. He never met a stranger, except himself. My daddy was about 5'11. He had medium built, a little closer to the heavier side, but fit. He was dark caramel in color, and had a beautiful smile, much like my mothers. It may have very well been my mother's smile, because a while hers began to dim, along with the light in her eyes. The ladies loved my daddy. I mean really loved him. But my dad's smile hid a very hot mean streak.

They say our behaviors are influenced by nature or nurture, which just means we are either born with it, or we learn it. I wouldn't know whether my father's behaviors were shaped by nature or nurture. He was left at the hospital as baby boy Grisaille. Janie and Mack took him in after being shifted home to home, at that point it was too late. I don't know when the anger or rage was planted, but it was evident that it had become rooted.

Learned Process

What is this world coming to?
Youth is lost
The paths they've crossed
Innocence lost
Disrespect their nature
Foolish creatures
Hating all they see
Parent figures
Ill mannerisms
Guidelines widened
Horizons shortened
All because youth
Isn't youth anymore?
No more opportunity
Just shut doors in their faces
All because of society
We can't blame the youth

We have to take responsibility
And blame ourselves
When they fight
Lash out
Hit everything in sight
A learned process
When they fuss
And every word is worse
And the curse
Remember it was taught
A learned process
When they break away from family values
And hate
Over the years
Installations of fear
Because of your inability to teach
Remember it was taught
A learned process
When family values no longer count
Wickedness
Massive signs of sickness
Remember it was taught
A learned process
Remember
Out of the mouth of babes
Comes truth
Truth
I repeat not lies
Remember a child sees all that is good
Men and fools introduce evil into their lives
molestation of the brain
Cropping and cultivating pain

CHAPTER 2: DADDY'S HOME

It's our best harvest
A child learns most in its early years

There were speculations about the man that initially raised my dad. I don't know them to be true or not, what I do know is that those unknown elements from his past would eventually alter my perception of love, worth, and would forever shape how I allowed others to treat me. I can't recall any good experiences in my childhood as it pertains to the man I referred to as daddy.

Across the street from my house was a little corner store. There was a dirt path that lay between that road and the store, and in the middle of that dirt path was a shack. It looked very rickety and at one time might have been some sort of storage shed. I can't recall why I was walking to the store by myself, or even what I went to purchase. What I do remember is that if someone had not instilled in me the warning of stranger danger, there is a high chance that I would have been the star on a weekly milk carton.

I remember it like it was yesterday, the one time I needed my daddy to protect me and he didn't.

"Hey," he would say. I would stop dead in my tracks. The hairs would stand up all over my body as if to signal fight or flight. I didn't know this man, but my gut told me something wasn't right about him. "C'mere. I wanna show you something."

If I ever questioned if God loved me and was real,

that day, God revealed himself and had angels waring on my behalf. I began to walk a little faster, and I flashed him a fake smile so as not to alarm him, and I said, "I'll be right back. Let me put this in the house. I promise, I'll be right back." Contrary to belief, I did use the good sense God gave me.

I ran home and told my daddy what the stranger said to me, and daddy seemed to be upset. He assured my momma that he would go handle it. He put me in the car and drove me to the store with him. All I could think was the way he beats on my momma I know he is going to kill this man for trying to hurt me. Daddy confronted the man. Daddy sat down on the bench with the man. And daddy and the man began to talk like old friends, and daddy, well daddy did nothing.

Till this day I wondered why he chose to do nothing. Why he decided not to protect me. I would now look at him like a coward. I would no longer respect him. That one single solitary reaction would forever change the way I saw men. The way I saw relationships. It shaped what I chose to look over and not address. That was the moment that I no longer valued myself, nor put faith in anyone ever again.

In retrospect, it could have very well been the moment that I had animosity in my heart for my mother's inability to protect me; to shelter me from the cruel, uncaring world. I no longer cared that she was in the fight of her life. What possibly could her childhood have been like to not have her maternal instincts kick in? At that moment, I decided I would be the protector for the twins. Domestic violence had tagged my momma a casualty of war, and she wasn't even aware of it.

One moment I would be laying on the floor of that beautiful little green house on my back with my legs crossed half Indian-style smiling, and giggling up at the ceiling. The next moment, I would be awakened by screams; horrible screams, earth-shattering screams; there would be broken glass, and the happy memories would fade.

There was a pounding at the door, and I heard my momma's footsteps running heavily towards the kitchen, most likely to get something to protect herself from one of the routine beatings. Daddy had returned home against the orders of the Clearwater police to claim his family. Only he really didn't want his family. He tried to instill fear into my momma. He didn't want her to be happy. He wanted to be happy, and to be satisfied with others, and there were others. He could have populated the earth with his others, and he did try.

If you are anything like me, you are probably wondering what in the world could possibly have been wrong with my momma? Heck, if I were on the outside looking in, I would have wondered the same. What would have forced her to stay? Did she have low self-esteem? Why hadn't she been enough? Was she enough? Enough of what? She could have been everything, and then some.

And he didn't care.

My momma loved daddy more than life itself, and he knew it. He was so sure of it, that on numerous occasions, too many to count, he would attempt to take life itself from her. He would use her love and forgiveness against her time and time again. He knew my momma was a good woman, and that she wouldn't cheat. He knew she had nowhere to go and no one to turn to. My momma was the oldest of nine children, and she had no one to turn to, let that sink in. He took advantage of her. He would charm her. He would beat her. He would coax her. He would kick her. He would woo her, and he would win. He would win, and we would lose.

We almost lost momma on numerous occasions. Once or twice a week she would have a bloody nose, a busted lip, or blackened eye. A hospital stay here and bruise there, this was our life. Sadly, this was NORMAL.

It seemed the more my daddy cheated, the more violent he became. I don't know, maybe it was the guilt he felt, or his inadequacy. Maybe he knew deep down he wasn't worthy of my momma's love, and he felt so worthless that he wanted her to feel as low as he did. It took me a couple of *forever's* to realize that hurt people hurt people.

I recall hearing the story of what happened after the twins were born. My mom was released from the hospital, and the twins were very little. Daddy got drunk, or that was the excuse that time, and was displeased with something my mother said. If I recall right, he got an inkling that momma had enough and that she was going to leave him. He came home with the usual "I love you," and "I will never do it again," attempting to woo her like he always did. Momma was fed up, and she wasn't having it anymore. She was going to take a stand. He asked one simple question, "Do you want to leave me?" Momma answered yes. She woke up in the hospital several days later. He hit her with a closed fist in the middle of her nose, and knocked her out cold. He then proceeded to kick her repeatedly in her stomach.

Apparently, the neighbors heard the commotion and called the police. They rushed momma to the hospital. She had to have an emergency hysterectomy from the extensive damage. She would never be able to have children again.

Hurtful things

Drama and trauma
And we're not even in E.R.
Confused as to why I allowed things to go this far
Feelings hurt
Tongues lash
Game spit
We bash
Each other
Each trying to prove the other one wrong
Ourselves right

SHE BLINKED: THE BOOK OF ME

We fight
Circling the ring
Throwing words like fists
Each one stings
Hurt
Jokingly you laugh
Wholeheartedly cry
But you don't see me
All you see is you
Why is that
Pulling all sorts of tricks out your hat
Just to be right
Fight no more
My heart can't take this
Sitting here emotionless
Stillness
When I should be roaming
Freely
Dearly
Nearly
Crying
Hurting
Am I dying
Loveless
Sleepless in Seattle
Like the cowboys herding cattle
Give a brotha' a rope
He wanna be a cowboy
Stealing my joy
With every twirl
Chipping away slowly at a piece of my world
Just to be right

CHAPTER 2: DADDY'S HOME

I'm tired
Fight no more
Love me or leave me be
Please
I repeat
If you love me
Show it
If not
Leave me not in pieces

It was moments like that, I would assume that caused the gaping holes in my memory. It was also most likely those memories that would cause me to long for Fantasy Island, Gilligan's Island, or any other island to escape to. We were safe for a while. The police had either rounded up daddy, or he fled back to Bronson. I didn't care which one it was. We had peace, if only for a moment.

Bam! Bam! Bam! There was a deadening knock at the door. He was trying to get to my momma. The setup of our house was very open. We had a screened in front porch leading to the front door made of glass. When you walked through the entrance and to the right was my mother's bedroom, and to the left, you would find the living room. Walk straight back a couple of feet, and you would see the dining room. If you chose to walk about two more feet, you would see the kitchen and finally the back porch. To the left of the dining was the family bathroom. We only had one bathroom, however, did we survive!

To the right of that bathroom is where myself and the twins slept. There were many nights when my momma had to run naked into the night to escape his fury. We would sleep lulled by the white noise of violence. This was our normalcy.

One night, my momma decided to stand her ground, she wouldn't scream, she wouldn't cry, she wouldn't run. She would hold her ground, and daddy, of course, in a drunken stupor and feeling sorry for himself, was coming into the house after what belonged to him, come hell or high water. Bam! Bam! Bam! And the sound of glass breaking everywhere. Daddy had kicked through the glass door coming after momma.

Something was different this time. Karma had found my address and was looking for my daddy. There he lay welling in a pool of blood. In his attempt to end momma's life, he almost snuffed out his own. In his effort to terrorize her he had cut his leg near a major artery and was bleeding profusely. She could have let him die. She would have been free, and she would have had her vengeance without raising one finger, but she showed no mercy.

Even at that moment, knowing that he was trying to harm her, she would not let him die. She couldn't possibly love him that much. Or did she? If she did, I couldn't understand it. She didn't let him die. She called the paramedics, and he would live to fight another day. I don't know if I could have shown such compassion at that moment, if I could be honest with you, without judgment.

I just might have let him fade to black and deal with his maker. One would think that would be the last time that he came after my momma, but it wasn't. He was relentless in his quest to destroy her, it seemed. It was as if he were on assignment. If he couldn't have her and keep his side chicks, nobody could.

In between daddy's disappearing acts momma would date. Nothing too serious. One thing my mommas dating life taught me was to be careful who you bring around your children. That is probably why I was so over-protective about my own, in theory.

And then there was Dale. Dale was an okay looking guy I guess. He could be charming, but then I was a little girl, so what would I know about charming. I am now realizing my momma had a type. Later in life, I would find that I also had a type. I don't know when it started, or how it started, but one after the other they would make me relive my nightmare over and over again. And they were so brazen with it.

I remember one night, I guess my momma had to work, and Dale was tasked to look after us. All I remember was him calling me into the bathroom with him. He was naked and sitting in the bathtub. He called me over and took my hand and put it on himself and he began to make noises. I was still too young to really know what was happening. So, I went with it. I knew it felt wrong, but I went with it all the same.

I don't recall him ever getting a chance to penetrate me. I wasn't going to give him the opportunity to either. He told me if I told anyone he would kill me. Somehow, I knew he, like my daddy, was a coward. Yet, I didn't want to bet my life on that. So, I waited patiently, anyone like that has a pattern. These types of behaviors are never a one-off.

Dale, like my daddy, was a cheater. He brought a woman in my momma's house one day, and that was my out! I waited for the right moment, and I told my momma. I'm sure I didn't execute diplomacy or tact in that moment, nor did I care. I just needed him out. He would not get the best of me, and he would not get a go at my little brother or sister for that matter.

If daddy wasn't going to protect us, I would have to. I developed a bulldog mentality when it came to my little brother and sister. I didn't care what you did to me, as long as they weren't affected. And I tried.

Question

You made me question who I am
You made me question where I stand
Am I a lamb?
Or am I a wolf in sheep's clothing
Made me question my strength
In Pain, I'd Always wince
From the stench
Of what I deemed failure

CHAPTER 2: DADDY'S HOME

This mailer
Once opened
Bust my bubble
Wrapped me in a bond of insecurities
The sea of forgetfulness
Wants no part of me
Daily I dream
That Someone
Anyone
Would rescue me
From what appears to be
An Eternity
Of darkness
All I need is
One spark that
Would ignite
The fight in me
The will to live
The ability to give
Second Chances
To withstand this
Pain that haunts me
Ghosts that taunt me
They show no mercy
Call cut the scene that reveals me
As the victorious entity
Yet luck escapes me
Leaves me weeping
Tears of blood
Can't sleep at night
The price is too high
You left me high and dry

And here I lie
I am facing my demons

I had so many questions, but I couldn't talk to anyone. Eventually, I guess my momma got tired of the busted noses and the black eyes, and she joined the army. She left us with one of her best friends, who happened to be the sister of you guessed it, Dale. God, however, had angels on watch because after that night I did not recall running into him again.

We were safe for a while. Donna had two boys, and I can vaguely remember their faces. I am not sure of their names. They were sweet boys, a bit touchy-feely, however, I survived. There must be a secret society of predators, and once you are marked as fair game in their territory, all you can do is pray, because all you are is prey.

I don't believe my mom was in the military a full year before I would hear the one single question that would shape my future, do you know this man?

"Hello little girl," I was awakened dazed and confused, eyes wide shut. The voice continued: Hon, I asked if you knew this man," I just sat there staring blankly at my dad. I wanted to scream no! "Nay," that's what my family called me, but momma was in the army, so I knew for a fact that It wasn't her. It was a man's voice much deeper. It was the voice of my dad. Since mom was not in the picture, he could claim us. He would later question me as to why I acted like I didn't know him; I never gave him an answer. Deep down inside he had to know. He would take us back to Bronson, Florida, a tiny town where everyone knew everything about everyone.

Bronson put the Kun in Country. Like any small town, it had its charm. Life was simple, everyone knew each other, and almost everyone was family. The city offered one way in and one way out. There were no big city lights, there was no movie theater. They had a high school, which was also an elementary and middle school. As a matter of a fact, they had two convenient stores, and a grocery store that was closed on the weekends.

Back then they had two channels, on and off. Well, I may be exaggerating just a little to lighten the mood. There was no nightlife, only heavily wooded areas and lots of hiding space.

Bronson also hid two jewels that no amount of money could buy. They went by the names of Mack and Janie Dixon. Grandma Janie and Granddaddy Mack were always the ones to smooth out the rough patches for me. In fact, they offered me a sense of safety and a sense of belonging. They allowed us to be children.

Granddaddy Mack

Strength
Strong tower

SHE BLINKED: THE BOOK OF ME

Power in the way that your voice rises and falls
Standing behind the pulpit
Or building a fence
To keep the animals at bay
Your way of dealing with life
Intrigues me
Empowers me to be
At one with the me
The creator intended me to be
You are the perfect man
That never existed
When pain came
You kissed it goodbye
Scriptures you read to me
Prayers you prayed for me
Somehow you knew what I was up against
In an instant
You covered me
You reminded me
That I was beauty
You fulfilled the duty
Of fatherhood
Father good
You were to me
And my siblings
Wiped off the dribbling
Of tears that smeared my face
With Hate
Self-loathing
You clothed me
In love
Kisses that I missed

That reminded me
What childhood should be
A net of safety.

In fact, they encouraged us to be kids, not young adults, not husbands, wives, or girlfriends, but kids. They made sure we were in church and Sunday school each and every Sunday. They took us on outings. They held us accountable for not doing chores. They encouraged us when we did things right.

They taught us the beauty of simple farm living. Most of the time the girls would be in the house with grandma, and my brothers Joey and Terrence would be outside with granddaddy doing man things.

Whatever man things were. I'm sure it included feeding the chickens, and cleaning out the chicken coup, collecting eggs, and such. As safe as I would feel with my grandparents, I never fully let me guard down.

Life in Bronson was a very intense period for me. It was the time in my life where self-loathing became a staple for me. I lost weight, people attributed it to me playing sports. It wasn't the sports. I signed up for the basketball team and the volleyball team and attended every game. I went to every practice even though I didn't play.

The reason I didn't play is that I knew it would require my daddy to sign a permission slip and forms. I didn't want to ask him for anything. I didn't want to owe him anything. No quid pro quo here! My hygiene began to be a problem. It wasn't that I was an unclean person. It was a defense mechanism for me. I can't even begin to fathom what was going through my daddy's mind. I actually believe he thought I was his girlfriend, or an extension of my mother that he could control.

I was young. I was helpless, and who would guess that the man that was raised by, the preacher, was taking advantage of his own seed. I would be awakened by soft touches in the night, and I would just lay there hoping it would stop. It didn't end. I still have reoccurring nightmares to this day. I try to shake it off and move on. Operative word being try. He wouldn't touch me while I was in the main house, at least I don't remember if he did. There are so many gaping holes in my memory. At times, I want to know what took place and when it all started. Sometimes I don't.

My grandfather owned, what I thought back in the day, a large piece of land. My grandfather partnered with Bronson Farms, he was an egg farmer. When you turned off the main road about half a mile on the right was my granddaddy's church, New Sepulcher Church of God. A few clicks more, and on the right side, you would see yet another green wooden house, it belonged to my granddaddy.

Before you turned down the dirt driveway you would see a smokehouse. When the chickens were no longer productive, granddaddy would barbeque and sell the meat. He made the best barbeque in the world. That was a taste you could never forget. His barbeque was legendary, and made with love, and you could taste it.

On rare occasions, we would get to help with the barbeque, and that would include wringing the chicken's neck, chopping off their heads, draining them by hanging them upside down on a clothesline, then sticking them in hot water which aids with plucking out the feathers. We would cut, clean, season and cook the meat. I was fearless then, and it was fun. If I had to do any of that now, I'd puke!

In front of the smokehouse was a fenced in area where the chicken coup sat. Once in a while, we would be allowed to help granddaddy collect the eggs. Living out in the country I started developing tomboyish ways, and collecting the eggs was something that required a soft hand. I would ruin more eggs than I would gather. Granddaddy would never get mad. I remember having to be very careful because granddaddy would set out traps so the wild animals wouldn't get to his chickens. I was a little wild and adventurous, and I loved the clanking of the steel traps when I set them off. Those were also fun times.

There was a muscadine grapevine, we called them bullets, separating the portion of land from the main house. When the grapes were ripe grandma would allow us to help pick them. She definitely had a green thumb, which was something that escaped me. Much like how granddaddy was the great protector, and that trait definitely skipped over my dad. Grandma was the reason I loved to bake, and would later be coined a scratch cook. In front of the grapevine was a medium sized mulberry tree and grandma would make fresh mulberry doobie, it was delish.

In front of the main house were roses of every kind it seemed. They were beautiful. That house too looked like love, and it was love. You could find my grandma in her wooden rocking chair at any given time. When she was there, a great conversation was sure to follow.

Diagonally across from the main house was where my dad lived. It was a small two-room structure. In the front was a little chair and a dial knob television. A curtain separated the two rooms. In the smaller room was a bed. The small house was close enough to be convenient, as it did not house a bathroom, nor a kitchen. It was far enough to be inconvenient, so no one would know my pain.

Anytime that I would have reoccurring nightmares it would happen at that house. It was as if darkness was trying to overtake and consume me. I didn't know that he, the man known to me as daddy was downloading a virus into me that would haunt and infect every relationship that I would have going forward. As bad as that time was in my life he was teaching me something.

He taught me to look for his behaviors in every man going forward. I was a virus being downloaded into hard drive after hard drive.

Infection

Infection
Looking at my skin
Is it a birthmark?
No, it's too dark
It's etched within me
Skin cream won't lighten
This thing
In spite of it seems
To live in the core of me
More often than not
It begins
To capture my attention
Not to mention
Sticks out like a sore thumb
My mind won't erase it
I request antibiotics to eradicate it
It seems to be resistant
In an instant
The physician
Diagnoses it
Insecurity

As I mentioned, I had poor hygiene, and I remember the moment I that I decided to use it to my advantage. One would probably raise an eyebrow at that statement. I know it sounds strange. The soft touches came more frequently. Maybe if I had screamed or said no, in the beginning, he would have stopped. I felt him slide next to me in bed and slide my small panties off, and he began to rub me. In my head, I screamed for him to stop. He didn't hear me, or he didn't care.

The next thing I knew I felt him separate my small legs and he began to perform what I would later learn was oral sex.

He would stop and ask me if I had a bath today, and I would lie and say yes. He would be sure to stop now; I hadn't washed my girl part in about three days. Unfortunately, that would not stop him. He proceeded to have his way, and then he got up to penetrate me. He decided to teach me something. I guess that was his way of rationalizing what he was doing to me. I recall him asking me if I felt that jumping in is private parts?

Reluctantly, I said yes. He then began to explain that was a signal to have whoever pull out. Was he serious right now? I mean really! He was advising me on how not to get pregnant, and I couldn't believe what was happening to me. I questioned why he could not have just called my momma to explain the birds and the bees to me like every other normal parent in the world.

How could he not know that hands-on was not needed in this situation? Time after time he would teach me lessons. He would teach me lessons in that shack, he would teach me lessons in the middle of the woods. He would teach me lessons anytime he wanted to, and I could do nothing to stop him. After all, who would believe me? On another occasion, he would make me sit on his lap, and his conscience must have started to get the best of him that day because he began looking for ways to rationalize what he was doing to me.

He had the gall to say 'you know you like it." I assure you, I did not. If I could trace the incident that started this series of events in my life that would destroy my self-esteem, and my understanding of what love was intended to be, I would have demolished it. Him or her! He must have held some kind of self-loathing and hatred within to want to destroy everything he touched.

I am pretty sure that I wasn't the only one that he did this to. I was so lost in this period of my life. I would start things and not finish them. Only whole things are finished. Something in my spirit told me to give up. Sadly, I got used to the fact that this was my life.

I began to develop a victim mentality and reverted back to a young child. I felt like a stillborn. Dead inside. I longed to shed this dirty skinned that clothed me. I started being what the elders called "fast". Meaning that I started acting like a woman before my time. I developed a flirtatious attitude. I was super sensitive and always emotional, and I wet the bed. I would cry if you sneezed in my direction. How did anyone not notice the drastic changes in my behaviors?

It was challenging for me to bounce back after that.

I was coined awkward. I was timid and shy around people. I would go along to get along. That is most likely where I developed a people pleasing attitude. My love language would now become sex. I would buy love and affection with sex. I was ashamed of who I was. And I would always wear a mask, mainly because I didn't want anyone to know what a hot mess I was.

When someone gets molested by someone that close to them, it really rocks your world. I read one day that there are 42 million survivors of child sexual abuse survivors in the US alone. They also say, "What is not repaired is repeated." Let that sink in! Another statistic reports that 1 in 10 children will be sexually abused by age 18. I was abused up into my teenage years. The most alarming statistic is the fact that 90% of the children abused KNOW their abuser.

Sexual abuse causes a myriad of problems, and long after the molestation ends they suffer from low self-image, some get addicted to drugs, some are addicted to porn, some begin to cut, some attempt suicide, some become the sexual abuser, some become introverts, and it leads many to question their sexual orientation. People often discount what gets transmitted during sexual intercourse.

Sexually transmitted diseases are sometimes the least of the worries. Now, sexual demons are a whole different ball game. There are antibiotics as well as homeopathic medicines available for STD and they are recognizable through medical testing. Sexual demons, however, can lay dormant in an individual for years before they realize it is there.

Sexual demons shred a person at their very core. They latch onto your soul and destroy any potential of having a healthy and productive relationship. I was introduced to my daddy's demons without consent. There was a study done that found male DNA in females' postmortem. Let's put this in perspective. When a woman connects with a man and becomes intimate, they create a bond. A soul tie or connection is made by design. That bond is designed to be an inseparable one until death do they part. Outside of that, confusion rears its ugly head, and things are out of whack.

My daddy could not have understood what he was doing to me, nor could any of the others that chose to take the same path. Or did they? To know someone intimately is to exact your will over another. That, to me, is a cruel and uncaring joke, especially if the victim isn't old enough or wise enough to understand the emotions that are required to enter into a sexual encounter.

Not only did I have to contend with my daddy's demons, but I had to ward off the attacks from the other women that his soul and now my soul were connected to. I would be handcuffed to his actions for years to come. I couldn't wash it off. I wasn't equipped to pray it off. I'd unknowingly search for my daddy's scent in every man that day forward.

Shedding

What is this?
Looking down at my hands
Skin shedding
Like my life
Fading away
Producing new
Revealing new layers
Stepping into the world

CHAPTER 3

AN ORPHAN SPIRIT

An **orphan** (from the Greek: ορφανος, *orphanós*) is someone whose parents have died, unknown, or have permanently abandoned them. In common usage, only a child who has lost both parents due to death is called an orphan.

A N ORPHAN IS DEFINED AS SOMEONE WHOSE parents have died, are unknown or have permanently abandoned them. Technically, I, nor any of my siblings, were orphans. Technically, momma left us in the company of someone whom she trusted when she joined the military. I speculated that was the only place she could run and feel safe. Now that I think of it, my dad's reach must have been pretty intense for my mom to think the only safe place to hide was the military. Well, they did have all the artillery she would need to be safe. Yes, I would say that was a brilliant move. Check and mate! Daddy was there in the physical sense, but emotionally he was missing in action.

I have to remind you that there are gaping holes in my memory for obvious reasons. One of my very first memories that I could vividly recall would be of my preschool years. Back in the day, they called it Head Start. Head Start was a program for low-income families; it would give children a chance at a brighter future. I don't remember anything about my journey in head start, but for some reason, I could remember graduation day like it was yesterday. I would wear my little cap and gown, and I would get passed over for a snack.

Now I could see how that could happen, and the probability that it was done out of malice or intent is highly unlikely. Nevertheless, I would begin to cry, and no one would notice my tears. Eventually, the oversight would be rectified, and I would get my snack and what I thought was the end of the world, would only be the beginning of a lifetime of pain and suffering. Unjustified pain and suffering, and I would blink.

Maybe my tears were the first cry for help. Maybe my tears were a sign of me lashing out at humanity for being anything but humane to me. During that period of my life, I was overly emotional. It boggles my mind how that escaped anyone's attention. I could recall weeks before how I got scolded for telling my teacher that my grandmother had died. I really loved my grandma, she was good to me. I don't know why I would attempt to kill her off in my mind.

Thinking about it, it was bizarre that I would even imagine that. I honestly don't know where I got the notion to make that up. Sad as that may sound, maybe I felt I was no longer getting the attention that I received before the twins were born. Maybe daddy wasn't around that much, and as wrong as our interactions were, I guess I just wanted some attention. I just wanted to be noticed. I was noticed.

My momma punished me, and that was that. I don't remember her asking questions though. I really wished she would have asked questions. I know I have questions just recalling this incident. Was I wishing she was dead? At the time I didn't know that she wasn't my dad's real mom. Maybe if she hadn't been born, he wouldn't have been born and I...I wouldn't have been born. Was that my way of burying a piece of myself? What could have caused me at such a young age to say such things? It was the beginning of my other reality.

To tell the truth, I probably saw something like that on an episode of Fantasy Island or one of the many other sitcoms I would get lost in. Anyway, I didn't account for the school calling my momma to send their condolences. I didn't entirely work through all of the details in my mind. I was only in Head Start! *Give me a break.*

How does one develop an orphan spirit you might ask? This is my theory. Please realize that I am not certified in this area per say. I can recall being pitied because neither my mom nor dad was around at times. I would notice grown-ups in my family give me the puppy dog eyes, and handle me with kid gloves often. We were shuffled from house to house and we never really fit in.

The only sibling that really had any stability was my brother Joey, and that was due to my granddaddy and grandma in Bronson. Taking a step back, being a carrier of the orphan spirit was inevitable for me. I would later learn that my grandmother threw my mom out of the house when she was around 14 years of age.

My mom would be sent to live with a distant relative, and she would be victimized just like me. The family member she lived with even attempted to prostitute her, and she ran away. She was homeless as a teenager. It really puts things in perspective for me now. My daddy was left at the hospital as a baby. He was tossed from home to home, it was said he was a handful.

As he got older, his reckless behaviors would cause others to want no parts of him. I didn't stand a chance. With that type of setup, it's a miracle I wasn't addicted to a controlled substance or a sex-crazed maniac.

For years I was secretly angry at my mom for not protecting me. Had I known her struggles, I might have been a tad bit more forgiving. No wonder she gave my brother up. Wait, that sounds so harsh. Let me rephrase that and cut her some slack. Lord knows, life never did.

Now it makes perfect sense why my mom and dad would gravitate to each other. They had the same spirit.

One of abandonment and lack. Each were grasping at straws for a glimpse of hope, and anyone to show them, love. The problem is neither knew what real love was and what it took to keep it.

Each had faced their own version of childhood trauma, and now they found comfort in the dysfunction of each other. My momma was the black sheep of the family, and now it all made sense. It would now click as to why holidays and family were so important to her. It was important because she didn't have love reciprocated in her past environment, so she set out to create that which eluded her.

He would not know his birth mother, and now my mom would become mother, sister, aunt, and everything to him. Maybe it was the abandonment issues that caused him to lash out with unbridled fury at my mom. Whatever the case would be, I and my siblings were screwed royally.

My siblings and I would be thrust out into the world without a covering. We would be naked and afraid. I'd often wonder what Joey's life was like? He had two parents in the home. He grew up in the church, and he had the spiritual covering of my grandparents. He also held animosity for my momma that he rarely discusses.

Maybe the grass wasn't greener on the other side. Something tells me I will never know. I won't even attempt to hold my breath due to the simple fact that I would only end up suffocating.

Holding

Hold on
I'm tired of holding
Conform
I'm tired of you molding me into another you.
Let me be me
The me that I am
The me that I was
When God created me
From a single grain of sand
That turned into many
The sins of the world
Upon me
Began when we
Stop
Breathe
Die
Live
See holding
Silence again
Where are my friends
When I need them
Yet I keep holding
There you are controlling
My every movement
Marionette style
Puppet on a string
Can't scratch the itch
My hands are tied

My brain begins to twitch
But I can't think for myself
Because I'm holding
And for what
Can't fight this feeling in my gut
That something isn't right
I try to fight this battle
But it's far too rough for me
I need help
Strength
So I lean towards you
And you
Put me on hold
I can't believe this shit
I hit my head against a brick wall
And all I get are more bruises
Open wounds collecting salt
Stinging
Pain
Holding another day

I carried that orphan spirit straight into my adulthood years. I never truly fit in, even though I was popular. I would be classified as exotic, strange, or different. I never really wanted to get too close to anyone because I did not want to be found out. I was a fraud. I had two parents that didn't know how to love me. I had a father that didn't take care of me. He didn't even want to pay child support to my mom, and she would struggle to make ends meet.

On the outside, I was this well-rounded kid. However, I was a little dirty, and a little smelly at times, but I was smart, and I had a nice body. None of those things mattered because the orphan spirit ruled my life. I recalled watching the movie called *Annie*. *Annie* was a movie about a little girl who was left on the steps of an orphanage as a baby. The only token that she had to cling to was half of a tarnished heart-shaped locket that once represented her family. She was a ward of the state and Mrs. Hannigan, played by none other than the Carol Burnett, was her nemesis.

Even though Ms. Hannigan gave Annie the business, she loved her in her own way, which I suspect was the only way she knew how to love. She was hard, sloppy, and a drunk. She embezzled money from the orphanage and was loose with the men, but to Mrs. Hannigan, Annie was family, and when it came down to the wire, she helped save Annie's life.

Annie was a cute little red-headed girl with lots of hope and spunk. She always stood up for the underdog. She was charismatic, bold and brave, and she didn't allow her current situation to stop her. Well, in true fairy tale fashion she was selected to spend a week with one of the most influential businessmen of the era, Oliver Warbucks played Albert Finney.

Mr. Warbucks, who stood 5'9 tall was a hard man, who prided himself for starting at the bottom of the totem pole, scratching and clawing his way to the top. He was all business and brawn, and he thought he was getting a little boy that he could teach business! He had no time for foolish things like family, love, or fun! Well, in walks Annie, played by Aileen Queen, full of life and song, then rearranges his entire life.

Annie convinces Mr. Warbucks to take a break from work, and they end up going to see Casablanca at the movies. The night concludes with Annie falling asleep at the theater, Mr. Warbucks picking her up in his arms, tucking her in bed, which makes him begin to question what is truly important in life, then Mr. Warbucks morphs into Daddy Warbucks.

Annie wedges her self into his iron-clad heart and ends up being adopted and she Daddy Warbucks and Ms. Farrell, played by Ann Reinking. They became the family that she, Annie, had been searching for the last ten years of her life.

The thing that stuck out to me the most about the storyline is that Annie nearly lost her chance at happiness holding on to a past that she knew nothing about. Her parents had died, but she held on to that locket for dear life in the hopes that she would have the family that she never knew. Mr. Warbucks even went to Tiffany's and purchased her a new locket, but she refused it!

It made me think about how strong and confusing that the orphan spirit is. That very spirit has convinced me to miss out on so many incredible adventures and people in my life for one reason or another. The orphan spirit has been stealing joy, marriages, friendships, and relationships for centuries. And will continue to do so until we confront it.

The orphan spirit will make you stay in unhealthy relationships because you feel unworthy of real love. It will cause you to by-pass real love because of the suspicion that something will eventually go wrong. It will ultimately leave you alone, confused, and depressed!

Busted and disgusted was the way that I walked through life. I didn't belong anywhere, and I longed to fit in somewhere. I would form friendships and relationships that were one-sided and unequally yoked, and I would be content to have anyone near me for the sake of having someone. To be honest, at times, I find that spirit trying to worm its ways back into my life.

I am cautious and watchful in my adult years. I will allow you into my space with caution. I really wish I had learned this lesson earlier in life, it would have stopped me from unwisely spending my emotional currency on those who didn't see my value.

Friendship was rare for me. True, authentic friendship that is. I carried leeches for years, and they sucked the blood, life, and tears right out of me. My power was destroyed by their kryptonite in the form of lies, empty promises, ill intent and fake love. They would wind me up, sit back, and laugh at my expense.

My foolish kindness would be taken for weakness time and time again. I would allow it all for the sake of belonging. I now know what the children of Israel felt like wandering through the desert all of those years. A trip that should have taken 2 weeks took 40 years. The absurdity of that is ridiculousness in its purest form. Yet, I wandered aimlessly with aching feet and an aching heart.

People would pity me, and I would accept it. They were creating a monster, a monster that would crave attention, any kind of attention, a monster that would lay down and be a carpet; a show pony, and a fantastic, beautiful disaster. They were teaching me how to be a victim, and boy, did I play that role well.

Don't get me wrong, I am not saying that you can't share the things that are attempting to break us in life. We can, in fact, it is healthy to talk about those things or people that hold us in bondage. It is very liberating. If you were anything like me, I was groomed to lay in my pity like a hog in mud, and I got really comfortable in the mess of my life. I was serving up a fresh dish of entertainment to those members of my family and community circle that coined my momma the black sheep, and they loved it.

It was, and is hard to break away from that mentality, and it takes a real concerted effort. I've learned that sometimes people don't want you to break free of those types of chains, because the moment you do, they have to focus on their own evil. Be mindful of the people in your life that are quick to throw you a pity party. I know I am now.

There is a quote by Frederick Douglas that states,

"It is easier to build strong children than to repair broken men." That statement is powerful! If we lived by that mantra, we could correct the trajectory of the lives of billions of men, women, and children who are under the spell of the orphan spirit right now! I can't count the numerous adult children in buff bodies wandering the earth aimlessly today.

Love conquers all! Those three little words arranged precisely in that order can correct any behavior in my opinion. If you have an unruly child, love them, they are seeking attention and love the only way they know how. If you have a teenage boy or girl who is displaying promiscuous behaviors, love them into submission. Most likely they have been introduced to a perverted version of love. If a person has low self-worth/esteem show them love via positive affirmations.

If you are dealing with a mean-spirited person or someone who is always angry, consider the fact that they have never seen true love in action. I know that the times that my momma was able to show us true agape love, it was a fantastic feeling. Actually, it was the best feeling in the world. Everything else in the world paled in comparison to her love. It was like returning to the safety and comfort of the womb.

I belonged there. There was hope there. I was close to her, and the rhythm of it kept me alive. You ever wonder why babies cry when they are born? I speculate because they experienced a love so rare and real, that being torn from the womb was earth shattering to them. That is how I felt when my momma left me and went into the army.

I experienced loneliness and a void that only my momma could fill. And for the first time, she wasn't there. She did not know that in her attempt to save her life, in my eyes she was killing me. I loved my momma, and in my precious little mind she was feeding me to the sharks, and they were hungry for blood. My blood. I was alone.

Lonely Is Only...

Lonely is only
In my head
Lonely is only
In my heart
Lonely is only
One word that consumes me
Before nature takes hold
And blooms me
Like the flower that I am
Lonely is only what pollinates me
The stinging feeling of love
Buzzing over me
When will this loneliness end
Or will it devour me
Spiral me and send
Me away
Like broken kisses in the wind
I want to scream

Yet no one hears me
Like silent beings
In an unscripted movie
Picture me perfect
Unearthed by calamity
Disaster is in my DNA
Handcrafted perfectly
Befitting for me
To remain unhappy
Lonely is
Lonely stays
Lonely craves
My attention
And I yield
To its vision

Since Conception

I've been searching since the day I was born
Since Gabriel blew his horn
To announce my arrival
Survival
My departure
The archer strikes a mighty blow
To the inanimate organ
Animating my departure
Pumping slowing then speeding up
Erupts like a volcano
Then stops
Hops. not skips a beat

Envy of self
Now the whole of me
Self-loathing
Not recognizing the beauty
That is inside of me
Can't get past the images
My eyes reflect back to me
Hidden on the larger screen
That consumes me
Tells me in not worthy
The pain that hurts me
Is it normal?
Conventionally as it is deemed to be
My future

Fu·ture: the time or a period of time following the moment of speaking or writing; time regarded as still to come.

I didn't know what the future held for me. To tell the truth, I didn't care, and truth be told I didn't care if I ever saw the future. Everything that I ever needed had enlisted in the army. I must have been a burden for my momma to have left me. I don't know what I did to betray her love and trust, but I would have done anything to get her love and time back.

I wish I had learned the craft of penning back then.

The words I have learned are compelling. Everything that I now see has been spoken into existence. If I had known I would have spoken my momma back home, back in our lives, and I would have pronounced her happy, healthy and wealthy so she would never have to leave us again.

My aunt ended up with us somehow after our stay in Bronson, Florida. We would be back in Clearwater. I guess daddy got tired of us. It was probably the fact that he could no longer control momma. He no longer held power to keep her fearful. She was much stronger now. That little 5'3 frame had developed a backbone, and she wasn't taking anything from anyone.

As I stated before, I developed a fighter spirit. My goal was to protect my little sister and brother from any predators. Unfortunately, I grew a false sense of security. I should have been watchful. I should have been mindful. I was lulled into submission by the freedom of childhood, and I took my eyes off of the twins and history would repeat itself, and my sister would become a statistic.

Remember that 90 percent of molestation survivors knew their molester.

My aunt married my molester. He was known to all as Ham. I remember my little sister asking a group of us what a virgin was. Jokingly, I said, "Something you're not" She was caught having sex with a little boy in the neighborhood.

Later I would have a conversation with her about the incidents and where and when it happened. Based on our discussions, the only good thing that came out of the entire situation is that Ham never penetrated her. It was mostly inappropriate touching and threats. Those cowards love to threaten their victims. They like to prey on the weak and the awkward. I asked her why she didn't ever tell. She stated that he said to her that if she ever told anyone he would kill me, my mother, and my little brother. My sister, like me, held it inside and died slowly.

It didn't dawn on anyone to ask her where she learned those behaviors. It was just another reason for them to pity us. Ignorant little mother and fatherless children. The Orphans.

Pity Party

I'm sorry, but I refuse to live up to your expectations of me
I can no longer look through the lenses you crafted for me
I can no longer pulse my heart to beat at your rate
I can no longer accept the love that is really hate
You hate the fact that I'm me
You hate the fact that you can't mold me
to be a mirror you
I choose to overlook the things you do
The things you say
The way you manipulate me to respond a certain way
You see you don't see my value
You keep shooting arrows
Those fiery darts trying to pierce my heart

SHE BLINKED: THE BOOK OF ME

See you're pretty smart
But I'm smarter
I was built to go farther
And you're just a mile up the road
You can't carry the load
That I'm carrying
These feelings that I've been burying are trying to surface
But you don't deserve this
This being my time
Studying the lines, you're trying to feed me
See I'm not hungry
And your soul is empty
You try to belittle me
While pretending, you're helping
All the while seeking to devour me
The news you see is
That I have power
Even if it's down to the 11th hour
He will rescue me

CHAPTER 4

Different

Dif·fer·ent: not the same as another or each other; unlike in nature, form, or quality.

'VE ALWAYS KNOWN THAT I WAS DIFFERENT. AS A MATTER of fact, all of my life I have heard people describe me as unusual, strange, spooky or peculiar. Even my children would be described as different. I don't know if that's a backhanded compliment or if that is a good thing, but hey if the shoe fits, I wear a size ten.

First of all, I have always surrounded my self with a diverse group of friends. My circle in high school alone would make you do a double take. There was Terry Roberts, the red-headed, quirky Irish guy with the most incredible voice. I secretly had a crush on Terry which really wasn't a secret at all. Terry grew up to be an amazing lawyer.

I remember, one day, Terry and I were hanging out at his house. I wanted so badly to tell him that I had fallen for him, but I was afraid of rejection. I was scared of what people would say if I were in an interracial relationship. And knowing me, my past hurts would not have allowed that to end well. My mom loved Terry, and it would not have been a problem with her at all. It was the others that I was concerned about. I always felt as if I were underneath a microscope always being examined.

There was Jayson Lazaro, he was Filipino and an amazing dancer. Back in the day, he had a group called inverted pyramid. He was the choreographer and mastermind. It was quite impressive to watch them dance. Jayson moved to New York after high school and went into fashion design and even ended up with his own jean line Lazer.

There was Michelle Smith, who also had an amazing voice. She was quite tall, and I loved her family. Definitely a blonde bombshell. And back in the day, Michelle and Terry used to date. They really were a cute couple that is probably the reason why I never made a move on Terry, that and the fact that I didn't think I deserved him. Michelle followed her dream and studied music and is now an opera singer and does vocal training.

Then there was Ray Long. Ray had to be one of the kindest, most loving gentle giants you would ever meet. Mama really liked Ray, and she was always trying to convince me that Ray was the perfect guy for me. I can't help but laugh out loud when my first son was born, how she was convinced it was Rays because my kids were so fair skinned. As a matter of fact, when Nick my first was born, the entire delivery room got eerily quiet when he popped out. Even the pediatrician on duty told me that my son wasn't fair skinned, but white.

There was Tammy Katsanakakis, I probably spelled that wrong. As a matter of a fact, I know I did. Tammy was Greek, and I remember going to her wedding, it was beautiful. The culture was amazing, and the food was out of this world. She got married shortly after high school, which I didn't understand. For me, life was just beginning. If she liked it, I loved it.

There was Mike Stephens, Michael Loberg, Amy and Micheal Burch, Lori Eichelberger, Shannon Daniels, Moe Daniels, and many others. The one thing that connected us all was our passion for music. It's extremely comical how I ended up in chorus. I was shoved into singing. Now, I used to sing in church when I lived in Bronson, Florida, but it was nothing like the formal training I would receive in middle and high school choruses.

Flashback to Middle School at John F. Kennedy in Clearwater. I remember wanting desperately to play an instrument. I am a natural and had been told that I have perfect pitch. Well, see what happened was… (buckle up y'all) I walked into the band room to audition. So, the band director, I can't remember his name to save my life, proceeds to tell me that if the note is high point up. If the note was low point down.

Don't judge me on what I am about to tell you. Well, I didn't know what the heck he was talking about and was too embarrassed to ask what exactly he meant about high and low notes. By the time we finished the audition he politely took me by the hand and dropped me off in the choir room and never said one word. He thought I was tone deaf.

I laughed so hard when I figured out what he was talking about. That one moment changed how I viewed and heard music from that day forward. It was also kind of frustrating because I to this day I do not know how to read music fluently. That one ignorant moment in my life would create a love for chorus, and that's how I met my tribe. It would also teach me a very important lesson, ASK QUESTIONS!

I should have remembered that lesson when I began dating and got married, but that's another book altogether! Yet and still, choir is where I met the misfits who would one day rule the world. They were a bright spot in my high school years. Definitely one of the more lighter seasons in my life, and not because most of my peers were white either.

I went to a predominantly Caucasian school, there probably were a hundred blacks that graduated from my class of 91. I didn't do cliques, so I branched out to see what I could learn from others. And boy did I learn! One would think that choir kids and so-called band geeks sat around all day and wrote symphonies. On the contrary, they were some of the wildest friends I ever had.

I remember this one time we had a sleepover at the Eichelberger's. There had to be about fifty of us spread all over the place. Some, I am not naming any names, could put down a few. Another time we had a party at Rob Vandaveer's home, it got kind of wild. Kids all over the place. Look, white kids really know how to party! There were street races, tubing down the river, where incidentally, I was introduced to the joys of sunburn.

That has to be one of the most painful experiences ever. I mean every inch of my body was burned—I literally mean every inch! When I walked, it hurt. When I bent over, it hurt. When I sat, it hurt. When I slept, it hurt! And then everyone wants to touch you or hug you. Let me tell you, I wanted to fight. Oh, and then to add insult to injury you peel, and it itches. No one warned me that the sun reflected off the water like a mirror. Dear white people, please educate me next time that I venture into new territory. (Laughs uncontrollably)

I can't believe people do that crap on purpose (sunbathing that is). Since then, I never went near outside water sources during the day. I had some amazing experiences like taking helicopter rides, playing dungeons and dragons. Yep, I said dungeons and dragons. My character was Glaciel, the ice princess. That was imagination at its best.

The game is such an adventure, I had to quit though because I felt some spiritual backlash from that.

Whew, I just got the chills. Dungeons and Dragons isn't for the faint at heart. A roll of the dice determines if you live or die. In a way, it's so much like real life. Depending on what you do today, it could have a lasting impact on your future. Sometimes life can be quite the gamble.

I loved my brothers and sisters from other misters dearly. The had a true and authentic love for me. All except one, who in a rage of fit decided to throw some racial slurs my way. Hey, there's one or two in every bunch. I forgave him although that is a learned behavior.

That would not be the last time that racism reared its ugly head. Heck, I remember when I finally started dating (I met him through a friend, he is like Voldemort to me. He whose name we should never mention) went to one of our high school chorus concerts. The guy I was dating got mad because Ray, the big teddy bear, hugged me and he started calling him a cracker and all kind of stupid stuff. I was mortified.

Some of my friends thought because I was dating the jerk, who I eventually married and had two beautiful boys from was influencing me negatively, and we grew apart for a while. I regret the day I met him. If I could do it all over again. I would have made better choices.

If I had a do over, I would have dropped kicked him to the moon. My friends valued me, and they loved me. They never cheated on me like he did with the most hideous girl on the block. They never let me work to support them while they did what they wanted. They embraced my differences and loved me unconditionally, and I needed that.

They opened me up to a whole new world of possibilities, I appreciate them for that. They were not the savior, but their love saved me at that moment.

In high school I joined every club I could. I was on the yearbook staff (Junior Marine Corps otherwise known as ROTC), chorus, and the African American choir. There was a silent rivalry between the two choirs. Our school choir director Mr. Knable didn't really think that the AA choir was as refined. I actually saw him smirk when we sang. In his mind, he thought it was amateur like. Simply put, he felt it was a joke.

I thoroughly enjoyed it. I lost a bit of my soul singing choral hymns. I don't think my vocals where blackish enough after that point. I enjoyed the diversity in each experience. I had the best of both worlds, and I would capitalize on that.

I loved watching what some would consider stupid movies. I grew up on movies like Pretty in Pink, The Breakfast Club, Who's That Girl, National Lampoons Christmas Vacation, Uncle Buck, What About Bob, Meet the Faulkers, 9 to 5, They Call Me Trinity, Arthur and Clue to name a few. Laughing again, one of my friends later told me that I watched red neck movies. It was the first time I would be referred to as a Florida Cracker.

I didn't care, the movies were funny, and I loved them! Truth be told, I thought EVERY black kid was watching those movies. At the time, there were not a lot of positive black sitcoms or films highlighting people of color. All that was offered was a lot of shucking and jiving, and I didn't want to see that! I wanted positive role models.

I was different, and my new-found family gave me the opportunity to embrace it. Don't get me wrong, I loved watching *The Cosby Show*, *A Different World*, *What's Happening*, *Good Times*, *The Jeffersons*, *227*, *Living Single*, *The Wayan Brothers*, and others, but I did not limit myself. I now know understand why. I would later find my passion to see others whole would require me to embrace all cultures and diversity of thought.

Love was color blind, and so was I. Unfortunately, I would receive most of the bullying from my culture, my people, people who were dark like me. I wasn't the token black. I wasn't tolerated. However, I was celebrated. I will say again, we are more alike than we are different. Society, however, focuses on our differences. We need to change that. Like, right now, change that!

I didn't date in high school at all. I wanted to date! It seemed as though none of the black guys liked me, not that I would have noticed it if they did. The brothers' skin would remind me of my daddy. And my interactions with my daddy ruined dating for every brother from that point moving forward.

I dealt with so much hurt and trust issues. My past was to blame for that. I was the none-virgin, virgin. I was sure that someone would find out that I was tainted and more sexually advanced than I should have been, and they would call me a slut, a Jezebel, or a whore. So, I kept me to myself. To tell the truth, had my prize not been unveiled early, I might still be a virgin until this day. As low as I felt about myself, I knew I deserved real love. Molestation stole that from me and replaced it with the orphan spirit.

Jelly (Jezebel Spirit)

Soft all over
Inside and out
No doubt
I just realized
I spread myself thin
Making commitments
To this one
This one
And now him
It couldn't have been the same me
From inside the mirror
She looks so strong
Edges so rigid
I touch her one time
And she cracked
Broken into a million of pieces
Then liquefied
No longer kept the original form
So she died
Life spread too thin

I would walk around aimlessly searching for a place to belong. It felt so lonely not being able to confide in someone. I remember telling my mom that I had been molested after she threw Dale out, and I think it shook her. She went into this tantrum of sorts. I asked her not to say anything, and she immediately called my aunt Joanne.

She said she couldn't believe it. She said she must have been some kind of stupid to not know. I'm unsure if she even remembered that conversation, but I did. It would be the last time that I would open up to her ever again. If mama had received that information better, I probably would have opened up about a lot of other things that bothered me.

In her defense, I guess that information would have been jarring to hear that you allowed a predator into your home. I'd imagine it would be alarming to find out that your child is now a statistic, she probably felt horrible at that moment. It is very critical that parents understand how they react will impact their child's ability to relate and share their deepest fears and secrets with them. My relationship with my mama was very different than most.

I longed to love my mama in the purest form, and I wanted her to love me. The love-hate relationship she would have with my grandma would not allow that to happen. She had her own childhood demons to face. She still has thorns that she needs to address to this day.

I wasn't privy to all the details of her childhood. I do know that her childhood wasn't a bed of roses. It was more like a crown of thorns, and a gown of poison ivy. There were definitely some generational curses, and cycles that needed to be broken.

I really wish mama had noticed my behaviors earlier and got me some sort of counseling. God knows I needed it. We lived in an era of "What goes on stays in this house." I am sure there were many like me out there. At the time I would know. I would struggle in silence and put on a fake smile, a mask of sorts. I'd pretend to be smarter than I was, and pray to God that no one would find out I was a fraud.

I was actually smart, I just dumbed myself down to fit in and fly below the radar. If anyone found out about the disease of the real me, I don't know what I would have done. I don't want anyone to think my momma wasn't a beautiful woman; she was, but my momma was hurting. I also know that the relationship with my grandma, her mother, was non-existent, and her dad, whom she barely knew, died when she was in the army.

Everything leading up to this point in my life was the perfect storm for the orphan spirit to be housed inside of me. Henry Fernandez once stated in one of his books, "If you want to destroy America, (or 'Merica' as it would be known), destroy the family."

I now understand why I wanted to hang out with

others that like me were different. They provided a camouflage, a covering of sorts. They wouldn't remind me of my past. And I would be free. I remember after graduating from high school going back and auditioning for the school talent show, which was pretty pathetic. I wanted desperately to fit in somewhere, and high school offered that to me.

It just dawned on me that I went to three different high schools. Like the orphan, I was shuffled from place to place, searching, not staying long enough to create any type of lasting bonds. Pinellas Park High provided me that safety, if only for a short while. I had protection in numbers, and they were my tribe. And I loved them all.

You embraced my differences
You kissed my misery goodbye
The instant you said hi
Hello to me
Greeting me
With open arms
Your charm was enough for me
To leave fear and disparity
Behind
For the first time in my life
I belonged
You gave me a song
And an instant family
You never took advantage of me

You showed me beauty
Ran deep beneath my surface
Love
You unearthed it
To move me into my destiny
Make me forget I was an afterthought
You dug deep at all cost
To remind me that I mattered
You didn't mind my rags in tattered
My brain being scattered
You rearranged me
Into beauty

I KNOW WHY THE CAGED BIRD SINGS: MEETING MAYA

High school provided so much joy that I almost forgot the beautiful tragedy of my life. Being different had its perks. I would experience things that others from my hood would not. One of the most pivotal experiences for me was meeting Maya Angelou. I was a senior in high school, and I found favor with my English teacher. She decided that because of the talent I displayed with writing, that she would take two other students and me to see Maya Angelou.

I really don't think that I was anything spectacular, but Susan did. I guess you can say that I was too close to the garbage that I considered to be my life, to see the message in my mess. She saw through the refuse and saw me, the diamond in the rough. I can tell you that listening

119

to Maya tell her story sparked something in me, and that something would resuscitate me in my time of need.

I sat there with my two peers and Susan, listening to each and every word Maya let drip from her lips. It was as if she was speaking directly to me. They say that tragedy is a catalyst for many things splendid. Out of the ashes, the phoenix rises. She would recant the story of how she was molested as a little girl by a family member, and how she wouldn't speak for years because of it. She also talked about finding her voice and how poetry pretty much saved her life. She had discovered her voice, and it was in that same spirit I would locate mine. I would find me.

I remember having my copy of her book, and I was so excited to meet her and have her sign it, and tell her how she and I were a carbon copy of each other. I would finally be free, and someone would know, and I could shake off the shame that held me hostage all of those years. I was almost free! I was ready to rip my mask off, and Houston… we have a problem.

I was so close and yet so far away. I would learn that Maya's mother was sick and she would not be able to talk to anyone. Her team scooped her up and ushered her out as quickly as she came in, and there I would stand deflated and defeated, and I would not get the release that I so badly needed. I would continue to be tethered to the spirit of the orphan, and I would continue to be different.

I wasn't sure what she would say that day, I didn't know if she carried the power inside of her to liberate me.

CHAPTER 4: DIFFERENT

The caged bird that was now free would not be able to release me.

Excuse Me

I see you have the keys
To release me
Please be kind
Find the time to free me
It's been an eternity
I've been walking around dirty
In need of a cleansing
These feelings have me trapped in
This dog pen
Returning to my vomit
Eating it up
Drinking from a dirty cup
My mind is made up
My mind is blown
Once again, I'm alone
The day won't end
I'm searching for a friend
A next of kin to erase
The curse when Eve ate the fruit
And Cain slew Able due to roots
Aesop's fable
Have me trapped within the storyline
I need an intervention
Of divine proportion
To clear the distortion

121

That is clouding my vision
Incisions in my wrist are calling me
My eyes are blocking me
From seeing the entrance
To my exit
I sit here vexed
And utterly perplexed
I thought you were my escape

Voice: the sound produced in a person's larynx and uttered through the mouth, as speech or song; the range of pitch or type of tone with which a person sings, such as soprano or tenor; express (something) in words.

CAGED BIRDS WHO DIDN'T SING

When you want to stress the importance of something, you repeat it. With that being said, what we don't repair, we repeat. I always loved being around my elders, and I have so much pride that my family has five generations alive to learn from. I am also glad that many of the generational curses have died along with some of those generations.

I remember I was blessed to spend some quality time with one of my elders. I will not mention her name, as her story is truly not my story to tell, but the stretch of her pain has reached beyond her years. I remember the night like it was yesterday. I had decided to throw myself into work as always, and she and I had been left alone. I loved being in her presence because her heart was so pure.

There also was a familiarity about her spirit that I recognized oh too well. She too had been victimized at an early age, yet the opportunity to hear her story would not present itself for years to come. I am unsure how we got on the topic of molestation, what I do know is that particular night she had a sadness about her. No matter how much she smiled, her light appeared to be dim.

We talked about our family and growing up in the south, and then she said it. She made the statement that she never felt loved, she never felt good enough, and she never felt like she fit in. There it was. What she was describing were the lingering effects of the orphan spirit. It had taken ahold of this beautiful, molasses colored complexion, white hair soul, and it did not want to relinquish its grip.

When I heard her make those statements, I was compelled to ask, "Well Auntie, what made you feel that way?" I sat and waited for her to reveal what I already knew in my heart, that she too had a soul tie with someone who would haunt her for decades. I saw her body slump, and she began to weep. My heart truly hurt for her, and I knew at that moment, that I had to share my story with her and let her know that she was not alone.

Now my aunt was one of the strongest women you would ever know. She was wise beyond her years. She was compassionate, and she would stand before me and weep like a newborn baby, and my heart would break for her. She would tell me her story, and she would wail. She was broken, and she would recant her story as if the event has just happened. I apologize that I cannot divulge the details as again, it is not my story to tell. Yet, that very moment shed some light on how the actions of those before even me would bleed into generations to come.

I understand that I could not take away her pain, or erase what happened to her, but I could stand with her and remind her that she was not alone. I could show her that someone heard the words that she did not have the strength to speak, and that I would be the voice for the caged bird that could not sing.

CHAPTER 5

Soul-Ties

Soul (sōl): the spiritual or immaterial part of a human being or animal, regarded as immortal.

Tie (tī): attach or fasten (someone or something) with string or similar cord.

DIDN'T MIND BEING DIFFERENT. IT WAS A MEANS OF escape. There were some things that different couldn't provide cover from. Things have a way of resurfacing no matter how deep you bury them. Rains will come, and slowly the erosion reveals what was once hidden. I would emerge naked and afraid once more.

The was the worst part of it all for me is that I wouldn't be able to attribute any of my failed relationships to myself. I was doomed from the beginning. Every sexual encounter would warp my sense of love a little bit more. I swore I wouldn't get into a relationship. I declared I wouldn't get married. I promised I wouldn't be like my mama.

There would be no way in hell that I would be in a relationship where a no-good man cheats on me and beats on me. There would be no way in hell I would lay with a man and not have my couple of forevers. There would be no way in hell, a sorry man would have me looking stupid in these streets! Point blank period! Not me! Never!

My first love did that and more. In fact, my first love cheated on me with the girl next door. Literally, the heifer lived next door to me! This was some bull... *Almost made me curse.* The thing that made this sting the most is that I told him about my past and he promised he would not take me through it. He took me through it, over it, besides it, and under it.

I should have known better, any dude that could sell a controlled substance to a family member was pure evil. I'd later learn that the same man, and I use the term lightly, would have his own flesh and blood selling for him. That was the thing that pissed me off to the highest point of piss-tivity. As I reflect on our hate affair, I remember at the beginning of our relationship I was going to break it off, and he started to cry. That was my out, and I didn't take it.

I have to admit, he wasn't all that bad in the beginning, and in the back of my mind I owed it to him to stay with him even in my brokenness and no one knows this to this very day that he didn't turn his back on me when I needed him most. I was right out of high school, and I went to a party with my cousin Rhonda. Rhonda was my first cousin and extremely beautiful. I had always been what you called a little on the thicker side. I was a brick house, but she was beautiful. And she was confident.

We met two guys at a house party in Largo, Florida, the guy was beautiful, and we slept together. I ended up pregnant. My first real time having sex, wild unprotected sex and I was now my mom. I was pregnant by a guy who I only knew as Rob. I didn't have a phone number, nor an address for Rob, and that probably wasn't even his name. All those so-called lessons from my daddy, and here I was pregnant.

I was afraid to tell my mom for fear of disappointment. I was scared to tell me cousin for fear of shame. I would walk around pregnant and tell no one. I would never have to tell anyone, at 5 months pregnant, alone in my downstairs bathroom I would experience severe cramps, my body would feel like it was being ripped apart. I would miscarry. I would have my first born in the toilet. I would flush, and no one would ever know.

That incident would be right before our family reunion in Bronson. I never really paid attention to the irony of it all. I gave my body to a phantom, and I would end right back in the place where it all started. I was so afraid as I was bleeding profusely. I didn't know then that I could have died from the amount of blood I lost. Again no one would ask any questions, and the loneliness would set in. The orphan gave birth to an orphan.

So many emotions come along with giving birth. Even if the pregnancy results in a spontaneous abortion. I was confused as ever. I didn't have anyone to talk to that wouldn't judge me. No one would understand how someone with such a bright future would be so dumb. Maybe if I had spoken to my mama, she would have educated me.

Instead, fear reminded me of my past and the time I told her about Dale, and I went back into my shell and held it all in. That seemed like a good idea, in theory. However, it backfired. Because I didn't address the emotions tied to loss, I threw myself into the relationship that every instinct in my body told me to run from, and I was pregnant again. For the first time, as far as everyone else was concerned.

This time, however, Clay and I would be adults and confront my mother about it. I imagined that she would be so happy about me making her a grandma. I was wrong, boy was I ever wrong. Instead, I got read the riot act, and she wanted to know how I could do that to her? To her? Really? I was the one that had to carry the baby. I was the one that had to face the shame of being an unwed mother.

I would be all alone, and I didn't realize that I would remind her of her life playing out all over again. My mom was twenty when she had me, and I would be twenty when I gave birth to my first. I let her down. I'm sorry mama.

I thought pre-pregnancy was the toughest part of

my life. I was wrong! I was now behind enemy lines, and I would be at war with my mom. We fought so much during the time that I needed her the most. I would resent her, and she would dislike me. I didn't mean to shame her. I really didn't. I was being a stupid kid having a kid.

Clay would stick by my side, and the false sense of security would have me throw all common sense out of the window. When I was about seven months pregnant, mom and I would get in this huge fight. I can't tell you what it was about, but she put me out. At 1 am, I would walk 3 hours and 3 minutes to stay at Clay's house. By the time I would reach I would be swollen and in pain. I am surprised that I didn't go into labor that night.

Eventually, I would go into labor and give birth to a beautiful 6 lb 8 oz baby boy he would be lovely, and everything would be right with the world. Shortly after I gave birth, my mom's heart would melt, and I would be welcomed home again. Everything was right with the world. Clay and I would fight, makeup, break up, and have another child.

Then the cheating began. On top of the deception, he would start to sell drugs, and then more girls would come, more fighting would happen, another child, and then finally, an abortion. I am not proud to say that. I was too much of a coward to carry and then give the baby up for adoption, so I took the easy way out. A trip to the bread and roses clinic in Clearwater and that was that. I was officially a murderer.

It amazes me the level of stupidity in which I operated in. Every single thing that I judged my mama for I had become. I finally got away from Clay, and the hurt would send me surfing the net looking for love in all of the wrong places. I was a wounded soldier and time, and time again, I would injure others. There was Tim, James, Alcinde, and Pete. There probably were more casualties, but I was in such a fog till nothing and no one mattered but me, and my flesh.

I was the afflicted, and I wanted everyone to hurt as I hurt! The good, the bad, it didn't matter. I was going to do me. I wasn't going to let the opinions of anyone stop me. Out of all the people, I hurt the one that stuck with me the most was James Hickey. James and I met while working together. I was his supervisor, and he was single.

At first, I paid him no attention. I was good and I was going to get my life together. I wasn't worried about a man at all. I was good. The more I spent time with James, the closer we would become. There was something about James that I could not shake. He was a true gentleman. He had no kids, he had a job, a car, he was super romantic, and he was white. I didn't mind at first, and I actually thought we were going to have our happily ever after.

James was about 6' tall with blonde hair and blue eyes. He was a handsome man. And Clay couldn't stand him. James had a heart of gold, and he definitely was searching for something. That's probably what drew us together. He was looking for someone to save, and well, I needed saving. James was actually the first man that ever prayed for me. He prayed for me. He prayed with me, and he loved my boys as if they were his own.

I would be the first woman to give him a child, and I'd also be the first woman to take it away from him. I hurt him so much. If only I had met him before Clay. If only my dad would have been a real dad. If only! James was the closest thing to perfection I would ever know. He would never take me for granted. He would wait on me hand and foot. He would love me unconditionally, and I would not know how to return that love. All I knew was destruction and dysfunction.

I was a natural disaster. A man-made natural, walking talking, living, breathing disaster, destroying everything in my path. I created soul ties and broke them, all because a soul tie broke me. I gave a love so strong it could cause a rift in the universe, and I took it back just as quickly. I want you to know that it was not intentional, nor by design.

The issue with loving James was the fact that deep down I thought he deserved better. Here I was a mother of two, and I felt like baggage. He was a very good guy. He could have possibly been my true soul mate. James was a virgin when we met. Many women were after him when we met, and he chose me. As I said he had no problems praying or serving God, and that was beautiful. I broke his heart and his spirit.

I remember many instances where James could

have run for his dear life to get away from the broken shell of a woman I was, but he didn't. He always went the extra mile for me, and I wouldn't at times cross the street for him. He deserved love, he deserved happiness. Instead, he got me. I recall one night I forgot, well at least I think I forgot to lock the sliding glass door that was on the side of the house and my ex-broke in and attempted to fight him.

He didn't want me at all, I now realized, he wanted to mend his pride. He must have felt some type of way to have been one-upped by a white boy as he would often refer to James. And James, he stayed with me even through that. It's quite amazing how the past will obliterate our future if we don't deal with issues correctly.

I would later search for him everywhere. I owe him an apology. I owe him life, and I owe him love, and I owe him his time back. Should one day you pick up this book, James Hickey, please accept my sincerest apology. I didn't know how to deal with comments from your parents. I did not know how to deal with the looks from strangers, and I was afraid that I would disappoint you, and true to form I did. I would leave you before you left me.

Shortly after my break up with James, I would attempt suicide. As diverse as my group of friends were and being able to love them unconditionally, I still wasn't strong enough to deal with the pressures associated with an interracial relationship. I thought I was failing at everything! I was a human pressure cooker about to blow because of failures in multiple areas of my life, taking advantage of people, not wanting to see my reflection in the mirror, and I would attempt to cut my wrist.

First of all! Let me say that cutters are gangster! Look, I made a small superficial cut and the burning sensation almost took me out. Even in attempting suicide I would be comical. Another instance where I was a coward. I should have known at that moment I didn't want to die. To cause pain to end the suffering. Now that's a theory. Yet people do it every day. If I may add, there has to be some sort of self-loathing in a person's heart to cut!

Dry Bones

I don't know
What I did to deserve
These dry bones
Bitter, broken and fickle
This tickle in my throat
Is causing me to choke
Everyone around me screaming stay woke
I kill myself for sport
And I put on quite a show
On the outside
I'm fine
From the inside
I'm dying
Blind
Looking for a way out

Of this minefield
With no walls
I go through withdrawals
In the absence of dysfunction
I have an unction
To offer my soul to the highest bitter
Re-tweet my love on twitter
For likes
On Instagram for bytes of sound
That will pierce my ears
On Facebook tears
Masked by emojis
Unfolding right before my
Eye spies something real
My true authentic self-emerges
The urges to disappear to self
I just might win

———————————————————

I wouldn't understand until later that soul ties worked precisely as they were designed to. As I began to study the bible I would understand Ephesians 5:31 the New International Version states "For this reason, a man will leave his father and mother and be united to his wife, and the two will become one flesh.

I can't tell you how many times I heard that verse in church, and it probably was more times than I have bones in my body. We need to do a better job of breaking this down for people. The first church is our home, and if we placed more value on biblical principals and the application of them, there wouldn't be half as many broken people out in these streets and in the churches as there are today!

I grew up with fire and brimstone teachings, those were good for a season, but what about the other seasons. We are also reminded that we were provided with everything we would ever need to gain wealth. I would ask that you, unlike me, would not minimize that statement. And these are just my thoughts, God was not only referring to monetary wealth. I wholeheartedly believe He was also referring to our mental wellbeing.

Mental health currency, in my opinion, is far more valuable than any currency in the world. The government can always print more paper. The mind, however, is not replaceable it can be renewed, but that takes a tremendous effort on our part. I would take me nearly 40 years of hitting my head against a brick wall for that to happen.

I didn't know how to get my mind under subjection, and low self-worth and low self-esteem would reign supreme in my life. I didn't realize until I forced myself to face all of the soul ties that would impact my relationships going forward. What started with my daddy wouldn't end there. It is incredible that I am alive today.

Flashback to 2000. I would move to Palatka, Florida to work with a rap group. That wasn't the only reason that I moved, but we will leave It at that. I moved back to the country, and that is where I met him. His name was

Horace Roynell Jackson. I need to make sure that I mention his entire name. Ladies, if you ever hear that name, RUN!

I swear, he was the younger version of my daddy. He was wrong on so many levels. If there ever was a relationship that was crafted to end me, it was this one! I tell everyone I know to this very day that each of us is assigned a guardian angel. Please understand, the enemy who tries to mimic God assigns each of us a demon. You can not tell me otherwise. Horace was that demon!

I remember the day we first met like it was yesterday. I was working in the Palatka Walmart, I transferred as a Customer Service Manager, and I guess they weren't expecting me to be African American and when I got there. They decided they didn't have any room for me. So, at my rate of pay, they kept me as a cashier. I would later learn that before I arrived, they would attempt to get the only other African American supervisor to step down.

I know. I know. Racism doesn't exist this late in the game, right? *Wrong* with a capital "W"! They would have transferred in a white male right after me, and he was able to keep his title. I digress, back to Horace. Horace came through my line one day, and he left me a note on my register. The handwriting was kind of sloppy, you can tell a lot about a person from the effort they put into their handwriting.

The note read, "Somebody like you," that was clue number one. Yup, I should have stopped there. I was alone in a new environment, and I wanted someone to hang out with. I should have gotten a dog! We would hang out with a friend I met named Ebony, and we would get close. Before I knew he would start spending the night at my place. He would soon introduce me to his father. Clue number 2.

Horace's dad was a piece of work, and he would do anything to gain his father's approval, clue number 3. Well, we went to meet his father, and I remember Horace and me sitting on the floor with our backs against the wall in his office. He sat in a chair looking down at us as to exact his god-like presence on us. Before we got deep into the discussion, he would order Horace to go to the park and take the kids with him, clue number 4. I should have run at this point.

Horace in lockstep follows his father's orders. No sooner than Horace backed out of the driveway, his father would make the statement that would shake me to my core. He would ask me and I quote, "Why are you with my son? You are more my type" I was like...what in the whole holy hell did this man just say to me? What kind of parent would be in competition with his son? Later in life, I would find this is more common than we'd imagine. I wanted nothing to do with him at that point. I would never tell Horace. Maybe I should have, perhaps he would not have idolized him as he did.

Horace like my dad was very sneaky. He was secretive, and I would later find out that he was a cheater. I was indeed stuck on stupid for him. He was tall, chocolate, beautiful, full of demons and sexually confused. I wouldn't find this out until later. I hate that I introduced him to my boys. One thing that I can strongly suggest is that you never introduce your children to a potential mate until its time! Time for me would be years later.

I would routinely ask my kids if he had ever touched them inappropriately, they would assure me he hadn't. I pray that is true! It would have devastated me had I failed my babies. I had met his dad, and now my mind would be stuck on seeing who in their right mind would have procreated with this fool!

Horace's mom lived in Cocoa Beach, Florida. We decided to take a day trip to meet her. She was not happy that I was dating her baby. At the time, I was 9 years his senior. Don't judge me, I told you all that I was going through some things. I remember standing outside under a tree where she and her friend sat. Under my feet was a palm leave branch and it was full of sand.

As I stood there, I felt something crawling up my leg. I was standing in a red ant mound. Well, instinctively, I jumped up, and as I did, I threw sand all over his mom's face. How embarrassing! This woman was probably adding up the strikes just like I did for her ex. The more the day went on, the more she let her guard down, and we would talk like old friends.

I didn't realize that there was a party in the works, and soon the yard would be full of friendly faces, young and old, enjoying the beautiful breezy day. People would come and go and I would assume they were all family. I guessed wrong. I went to lay down because the sun began to take a toll on me. I was later awakened by Horace's mom telling me that I needed to get outside and pay attention to my surroundings.

She would rat out her son for going into the bathroom with another female, while I was asleep, unaware and pregnant, yes… again. Once again, here I am doing all for a man that took my kindness for weakness and cheated. Months later I would be called to Shand's Hospital in Gainesville, Florida due to abnormalities with my bloodwork during a routine visit. They wanted to perform an amniocentesis to confirm their findings.

I would learn that I would be having a girl and I would also receive the news that I was carrying a Trisomy 18 baby. Research would later reveal that Trisomy 18 pregnancies occur in 1 out of every 5000 pregnancies and are most often females. There are three types of Trisomy 18 pregnancies. I won't bore you by going into the details of each. Horace, the boys, and I headed straight over to the hospital, and it was confirmed I was a carrier of the trait.

I was given two choices, they could induce labor, and I could hold her until she died, or I could carry her for nine months and then she would die. I genuinely think that moment and the anticipation of the months to follow pushed him slap over the edge of sanity.

Earlier in the day, we would be playing cards with friends laughing and joking, and that night I would be laying on the floor gasping for breath. Horace would straddle me on the floor and punch me repeatedly in the face. He would choke and hit me. I did not know where all the rage came from. I thought I was going to die.

This would not be the first time that there were signs that I should run for dear life. Weeks before I would be laying on the couch facing the fireplace. You know how you can be in a dead sleep and feel the presence of someone standing over you? I was laying on my back, and as I slowly opened my eyes, I could see the silhouette of a man's body standing over me.

I snapped my eyes open really quick. As I began to focus, I noticed him wearing a white tee shirt and it appeared to have knife knicks in it. Everywhere the shirt was knicked, you would also see what seemed to be blood. Boy did that grab my attention. All I could think was be cool. No sudden moves. I put my hands by the side of my belly to sit up and there it was the knife. It had remnants of blood on it, and I was terrified.

He handed me a letter and walked away. I should have packed up and left at that very moment. Later he would come after me with a knife stabbing the wall as he approached me. I guess he figured he scared me enough and he left me in the room. The first chance I got, I jumped out of the window and took off. I was reliving my mama's life.

I left my kids, praying he wouldn't harm them, and I went screaming into the night. He would quickly notice that I was no longer in the corner he back me into and he would run out the front door and hop in the car to come after me. Well, I circled back around and grabbed my babies and ran to the neighbor's house and called the police.

That night I think he planned to kill us, or at least me. I would come back to a broken front door, a broken bedroom window and fire scorched wall in the living room. The police came out in numbers. They asked if I wanted him arrested, I said no, and asked if they could Baker Act him. That was pretty much the end of Horace and me.

About 3 months ago, I was talking to God, and He told me that He wanted to show me something. He wanted to show me what He saved me from. He had me Google Horace, my jaw dropped. God saved my life! He had been arrested April 20, 2017, February 7, 2018, November 14, 2016, August 20, 2013, April 27,2013, May 28, 2013, for various reasons. I truly dodged a bullet!

I now understood why my mama wouldn't let my daddy die the night he came after her. From that moment going forward, I would never say what I wouldn't do, or put up with in a situation until I lived it. Mama, I'm sorry for judging your journey. I love you tremendously. Despite all that, my mom went through she would remain a beautiful soul. There would be other souls that I would be tethered to. No wonder I was so broken, so bruised, and at times so bitter.

Relationships like those I mentioned above created

soul ties in my life and those perversions of what love was supposed to be ruined many opportunities in my life due to a lack of trust. Any time a male figure came around, I would tense up, anticipating the worst-case scenario to happen. I remember being in high school in Bronson during my freshman year and Ellas McDaniel, known to the world as Bo Didley, invited me to his home recording studio, after performing in the gym of Bronson High School. I didn't go. I don't know if it was because I was scarred by wolves in sheep's clothing of past, or because I didn't think I deserved it.

Either way, Bo Didley was enormously influential in transitioning the rhythm and blues world to rock and roll, and I would dismiss the opportunity. He was said to have a significant influence on Elvis Presley, The Beatles and more according to Wikipedia. He worked with greats like Etta James, The Rolling Stones, Marvin Gaye, Little Richard and others and he wanted me! He would later die in the town of Archer, Florida at the age of 79.

Anyone in their right mind would have jumped at the opportunity. They would have asked questions to gain clarity. I was not in my right mind. Nor did I know how to be. I would miss opportunity after opportunity for fear of being judged.

I know that at one time or another I have judged those that judged me without knowing the extensiveness of the damage to my internal man. I fought every day to survive. And believe me when I say every day was a fight to the death. Because of my tether to my daddy, I had low self-esteem, I hated to see myself in the mirror, and I didn't take care of myself. I didn't want to be appealing to any other predator. I didn't feel like I belonged anywhere. I didn't think I was smart enough, at times I didn't try, I started things I would never finish.

I have hundreds of poems and unfinished works that I didn't move forward with because of those insecurities. I allowed people to walk all over me. I attempted to buy people's love through service. That would all change when I stopped focusing on serving man, and shifted the focus to serving God.

It's important that you understand I am not attempting to convert anyone. I do not have that type of power. What I need and want for you to understand is that we all have those secrets that we don't want anyone to know about us. God doesn't deal in secrets, and He is not judgmental like we are. I was judged harshly back then for my ignorance. I was judged back then for the soul ties that no one taught me about until it was too late.

Mama didn't have the sex talk with me I was naïve and green. Maybe she was uncomfortable. Whatever it was that discussion could have saved me from a world of hurt. It would have saved a lot of people from a lot of pains. I would not have relinquished my power and authority so easily time and time again.

I've heard some say that men and women couldn't be friends. I genuinely believe that is a lie. The unfortunate truth is there are so many warped perceptions of what friendship looks like. Today we call it friends with benefits. You can now think of it as friends with tethers. Tethers that tear. Tethers that bind. I used to hear people say don't hate the player, hate the game. Well, the game can be played if you know the rules. I shied away from the rulebook and dared to be upset when I lost.

For years my children dealt with that orphan spirit because generations before and leading up to me would never address it. We placed ourselves in bondage. We developed a victim mentality. We bled and repeat. Everyone by now should know the definition of insanity.

> **In·san·i·ty:** (n) mental illness of such a severe nature that a person cannot distinguish fantasy from reality cannot conduct her/his affairs due to psychosis or is subject to uncontrollable impulsive behavior.

There is the notion that doing the same thing over again expecting a different result is insanity. It is not. It may be a product of insanity, but the correct definition as defined by Psychology Today is a severe nature that a person cannot distinguish fantasy from reality, they cannot function in life due to uncontrollable impulsive behavior. Please remember this the next time you coin someone insane. I know I will.

To add insult to injury, many people do things

of their own free will and in their own agendas to claim insanity. Mental health is nothing to be scoffed at, made light of, or joked about. We all wear masks, some of the most dangerous faces hidden behind those masks are those of mental illness. It's a dangerous game of Russian roulette one can play if they suffer from mental illness and it is not correctly diagnosed by a health professional.

If mental health issues plague any part of your family, see a doctor and make sure you are okay. If it runs in your family, I urge you to stay away from alcohol and drugs. The substances have a way of amplifying our issues.

I would walk around wounded for many years. I was torn, and I was at war with myself. I was always seen with a smile, always giving advice, (which was very dangerous in my condition) always trusting people that secretly hated me. There was a time that I would hang out with folks that tolerated me because the issues in my life made them feel better about themselves. I would shift and go where I was celebrated. The conversation was very different there.

I wish I could say that the darkness would never come back to consume me again. I wish I could say that I discovered the pill that would cure me.

SHE BLINKED: THE BOOK OF ME

CHAPTER 6

The Absence of Light

Light: the natural agent that stimulates sight and makes things visible an expression in someone's eyes indicating a particular emotion or mood

"**K**ISHA, I NEED YOU TO CALL MY MOMMA TO come get my kids!"

"Renee, what are you talking about and what's wrong? Renee, what's wrong? Renee! Renee!" My family and friends called me Renee. I would begin to cry and mumble. I couldn't see straight for all of the tears. My head was pounding, and I was lost.

The only thing I knew to do was end it all. I tried to cut. But it hurt so bad. I saw a bottle of Benadryl, and I saw a bottle of Tylenol and some other random over the counter pills. One by one I could feel them slide down my throat and my body welcomed them. My kids were sleeping only a few feet away from me, but in that moment, it didn't matter.

I was worth more dead than alive, and they would be financially taken care of. My mama would get them, and they wouldn't miss me. You have to be mindful of what you speak. Words are powerful, and some times we take that for granted. I forgot that we were created to have dominion over the earth. For the last couple of years, I did everything but rule. I was the side show, the freak, the jester, and the ring leader.

My life wasn't all darkness, I'm sure. I would search for memories that would validate that but, at that moment, I could not capture them. I could remember how when I was young we would get some of the mason jars that my grandma used to use for canning and try to capture the lightening bugs. I know that is probably not the technical name for them, but like my life, none of that mattered.

If I could just capture some light, I might make it until morning. The word says weeping may endure for a night, but joy comes in the morning. The problem for me is that morning never happened. However, my friend mourning was always there to greet me. It never failed. I would hang up the phone and wait. I had a date with destiny, and my date's name was the grim reaper. I sowed so much discourse in the lives of others and myself that death at that point was just the friend I needed, so I thought.

The problem with committing suicide is that we rarely think about the aftermath. We rarely see that family would have to try and pick up the pieces that we left behind. We never think about the grief, the tears, the pain, and the costs that go way beyond the financial burdens. We just don't care. We can't see, we are utterly blind to those things. Well, let me speak for me. I recalled going to many funerals consoling or being consoled. There was nothing happy about them.

I was waiting to die. I would get really sleepy, and I would feel my body slip to the floor. I'm not sure how much time had passed. I would hear what I though was a faint knock at the door, but I couldn't react, I was so sleepy. I could hear voices all around me, but I couldn't move.

The only way could describe it was as if I was in a state of sleep paralysis. I could hear conversations around me, but I couldn't move. I heard someone scream oh my God, call 911. I was just so sleepy. I heard someone ask where are the kids? This is definitely tough for me to recall. Even though this happened years ago, it feels as if it was yesterday. There are so many emotions welling up inside me right now. I've already had to snap myself out of a trance several times.

This time, unlike others, I will face these emotions, and I will finish stronger than ever before.

I could hear the distant chatter around me, and I couldn't answer. I began to panic, but they couldn't see it, they couldn't feel what I felt. I thought I heard one of the paramedics say that they thought I had ingested crack, I wanted to cuss. I tried to defend myself. Just because I was in distress didn't mean that I was on drugs.

I had never taken illegal drugs in my life, let me rephrase that, I had smoked marijuana after my daughter's funeral. Someone gave it to me to relax me. It did, I forgot my troubles for a while. Other than that, no that wasn't my cup of tea. I do not ever want to ingest, drink, smoke, or shoot up anything that has the power to override my judgment. Weed made me too chill, and that would be the end of that.

They placed me on a stretcher, and they took me to the hospital. I vaguely remember them taking my bra in the event I wanted to hang myself. I guess it could be done if one wanted to be creative. I didn't have the energy to do all that. I was tired. I was barely getting by as it was. The thing I did remember, was waking up to seeing my baby brother standing next to me looking at me with so many questions.

Like I said, we rarely think about those we are leaving behind, and if we do think of them, it's only from the perspective of how much better their life would be if we were not in it. I could see the damage that I had done, by attempting suicide. Imagine what would have happened if I had succeeded. Thank God for failure. I didn't think about what I would have subjected my babies to. It was definitely a wake-up call. Soon everyone would be escorted out of the room.

I had an intake nurse ask me some questions at the bedside. She would ask me my name and some other information it was all really just a blur. She went out, and someone else would come in. I would answer questions like an automated service, with no life and no spunk. I had no energy nor the drive to be cordial or cheery.

Then it happened the nurse came into the room she was a heavy set older woman, and she had a cart. I didn't know at what point they put the straps on my wrist, but I was strapped to the bed, and a tube was being shoved down my throat. I wanted to fight, but it was useless. It felt as if they were trying to push it to the opposite end. I could be exaggerating a little, but hey, I had just tried to snuff myself out, so why think about care and kinder now?

I would hear someone begin to explain what was about to happen. Now, I am going to fill your stomach with charcoal, and if you throw it up I will have to do it again! If you have never had to have your stomach pumped, trust me you never do. They fill your belly with this black looking fluid that tastes like crap. I didn't expect it to taste like chocolate, I don't know what I expected, but that wasn't it. They would fill my stomach and use this pump like machine to suck it back out. They ran that cycle twice due to the number of pills I had taken.

I'm not very fond of pills to this day. I have to be in severe pain to take anything. Each day was a new day to try again. I tried to sleep my life away, and they wouldn't let me. Who knew sleeping all day would label me as depressed, actually, I thought it was because I was tired or just being lazy. I would begin to sit at home and I would pull the shades closed. When I was off, I didn't want to be bothered by anyone.

I began to be antisocial. I didn't want to go out. I lost interest in almost everything. Who knew that there was a clinical name to what I had been going through. Well, I was in the right place because they would not allow me to sleep all day. They would make me get out of bed even if it was only to sit in the common area and watch television.

I lost a ton of weight in those three weeks, at first, I wouldn't eat, and I would give my food away. I learned quickly, that would only prolong my stay. So, I started faking it until I made it. I really wanted to go home, but apparently, I wasn't social enough. What I did learn without a shadow of a doubt, is that there were three types of people there.

The first group was the *everyday Joe's* that kept holding things in until they snapped. We were the nice guys, the ones that lived to please others until all the steam would build up, and pop, and then, one day we'd go too far. We would only need to learn to communicate our hurt, and learn not to tip toe around our issues, as well as learn to put ourselves first.

The second type I saw there were the lifers, they would rotate in and out, trying to keep their benefits. There were two sisters in there that I could remember. I swear they would do off the wall stuff just to get attention. I remember sitting on the couch, minding my own business, so that I could get out of that psych ward. Along comes one of the sisters wearing this moo moo type night gown. She would sit in front of me and spread her legs with no underwear on. I was pissed. That was so disrespectful.

I really wanted to act of out of character and wrap my hands around her throat and choke the life out of her, however, I couldn't because violence was frowned upon. That, in turn, would have extended my stay. I wanted my freedom. I wanted control of my life. The irony of it all was that my visit was the beginning of my journey to freedom. It was the opening to a life of normalcy; a life without dysfunction or at least an awakening to what dysfunction was. For now, I had to play nice and get away from her and her sister.

I nicknamed them the natural disasters. They had to be told when to bathe and brush their teeth. They would go to the ladies' room and not flush. They were nasty, would pick their noses and always want to touch you. It gives me the *heebie-geebies* just thinking of them. Needless to say, I couldn't wait to get away from them. If I ever have to fake something to fit in, I'll never fit in!

The third type was the broken-hearted, the sunken spirited, the ones that dwelt far beyond the reaches of light. They had suffered so long that life to them was devoid of hope, they sat in the absence of light. Our rooms were a dorm type of room, and there were four beds in the room. There was no television and nothing to make it comfortable enough to stay in there. The staff wanted us to spend most of our days in the common area. The staff wanted to see us socializing. I didn't want to socialize, but I would try.

At the time there were only two of us in our room. My roommate was a beautiful girl. I cannot remember her name, we will just call her Jennifer. She looked like a Jennifer to me. She was a sweetheart. She was very quiet and polite, and she never caused any trouble. At first glance, I wondered what was wrong with her, and why she had been hospitalized. During the day she was semi-social, and she even laughed quite a bit. She never really went too deep into conversation. Truth be told, I didn't want to get too friendly with anyone behind those four walls. It was a time I wanted desperately to forget!

Nonetheless, she was the most normal person that I could relate to. Like I said, life with her as a roommate to me would be a piece of cake compared to the others. It was a piece of cake until night fell. Like clockwork, around 10:30 or 11:00, the quietness would be broken by bone curdling screams. Whatever happened to her must have been terrifying. The first night I didn't know what to do. I would lay there paralyzed in fear. She would scream, and no one would come.

I guess they were used to her screams and were somehow able to drown them out. I couldn't!

Every night like clockwork the episodes would come, and I did the only thing I knew to do. Motherly instinct would kick in, and I would begin to sing. I really wasn't singing for her at first, I was singing for me. I was singing to calm me down. I didn't want whatever had crept into her to spill over into me. I was attempting to keep whatever little light I had left burning. I was scared that if I crossed over, I wouldn't comeback.

I started thinking about life and how I deserved to live. I thought about how things were not as bad as I have envisioned it. I noticed the more I sang, the calmer she got. Her screams would simmer to a low dim, and then I got the courage to step over to her bed, hold her and rock her, and assure her that it would be alright. I wish I knew what "it" was. Every night I would sing to her, and each morning, I would feel a little lighter. I would be a little fre-er. I was self-healing, self-medicating ingesting positivity through hymns and old gospel songs Janie and Mack had taught me. What they had put in me was coming back up, and I was fighting back.

In one of the darkest times in my life, I was discovering the will to survive. I would wake up each morning and poetry would spew from my gut. I'd wake up singing, drawing, painting, and living. I would begin to smile. I would remember who I forgot to be before my innocence was taken. I would recall me before the loss, me before the one-night stand, me before daddy issues, the me I was created to be. Singing was my escape, and there was a healing spirit working inside of me.

I would later hear that my children's father would

voice that he wished that I had died. There were also some new allegations concerning my children that I would need to address. That in itself is another story all together. I pray it isn't true.

I'm sorry, but I refuse to live up to your expectations of me
I can no longer look through the lenses you crafted for me
I can no longer pulse my heart to beat at your rate
I can no longer accept the love that is really hate
You hate the fact that I'm me
You hate the fact that you can't mold me
to be a mirror you
I choose to overlook the things you do
The things you say
The way you manipulate me to respond a certain way
You see you don't see my value
You keep shooting arrows
Those fiery darts trying to pierce my heart
See your pretty smart
But I'm smarter
I was built to go farther
And you're just a mile up the road
You can't carry the load
That I'm carrying
These feelings that I've been burying are trying to surface
But you don't deserve this
This being my time
Studying the lines, you're trying to feed me
See I'm not hungry

And your soul is empty
You try to belittle me
While pretending, you're helping
All the while seeking to devour me
The news you see is
That I have power
Even if it's down to the 11th hour
He will rescue me

Grace: the free and unmerited favor of God, as manifested in the salvation of sinners and the bestowal of blessings; a period officially allowed for payment of a sum due or for compliance with a law or condition, especially an extended period granted as a special favor.

God would extend grace once more. He had saved me for a reason, what the reason was I wouldn't know for years to come. I would be lying if I said that the depression didn't try to creep back in every opportunity it could, because it did. I was better equipped now. I would learn that I was not the only one in my family battling mental health issues, or any issues at that.

I would also learn that I was not the only one in my family that fell prey to predators. What goes on in this house, stays in this house would haunt generations before me and after me. I said it once before, what we fail to

157

address we will undoubtedly repeat. I was determined to break the cycles. I was trying to save my sons. It's hard to save someone as an absent parent. I would throw myself into work believing that was what was best for them. Every time I missed a first step, or a birthday, I'd replace it with a Disney vacation, or a trip to the movie. I at times, wish that God's grace would provide me a do-over in some situations, but I bless God that His wisdom did not allow for a do-over..

CHAPTER 7

Waking Up:
Back To Life

I T WOULD TAKE MULTIPLE SUICIDE ATTEMPTS, THREE weeks in a mental institution, and seeing myself and others in various stages of dysfunction, and depths of mental illness to understand that I did not want to die! I wanted to live, I no longer wanted to hurt myself or others, and I could forgive myself for the sins of others before me. I couldn't take back any of the daggers that I threw in the heat of arguments.

I couldn't cancel the discounts I gave to others to misuse and abuse my body out of familiarity, but I could, from this day forward, make a conscious decision to love myself, and to assess and check my heart daily. I would no longer allow others to dump their failures and inconsistencies on me. I would fight every day to keep my head above water. Some days would be better than others, but I would be alive.

I wish that I could say that I got it right every time, and that I would not leave a trail of casualties in my wake, but I cannot. What I can say is that I started each new day with a clean slate. I gave myself permission to love and to be loved. I gave myself the authority to be great. I gave my permission to make mistakes. I gave myself permission to be the beautiful mess that was me! I left that mental institution taking zero medications. It wasn't that I was entirely healed by man's standards, I made the decision to be a victim no longer. I would face my so-called demons, and I would walk by faith. If the truth be told, I would have loved to change the channel on what my sight would reveal.

I would now be better equipped to deal with life. There is no secret sauce per say. Each of us has to soul search and find what works for us. What worked for me was grace and a relentless pursuit of God. I ran after Him like my life depended on it. We are all looking for something to fill the voids. Some seek others, some look to alcohol, some look to drugs, some gamble, but I ran after God.

Re·la·tion·ship: the way in which two or more concepts, objects, or people are connected, or the state of being connected.

Religion (re·li·gion): the service and worship of

> God or the supernatural commitment or devotion
> to religious faith or observance; a personal set or in-
> stitutionalized system of religious attitudes, beliefs,
> and practices.

They taught me religion; I needed relationship. I was raised in the church, and I knew religion. I knew to sing, wave my hand and repeat what I was fed. Religion never worked for me, but my relationship with God did. I wish that someone, anyone had taught me the difference earlier in life. I am happy however, that I have learned the difference between the two, and I now use my light to assist leading others to the one who can help them find theirs. I read the story of Adam and Eve countless times, and I never understood how generations before me would affect me.

Religion taught me that the sins of those before me would have me bound, and that no matter what I did, I would have to prove myself over and over again and that would exhaust me. Relationship taught me that God would carry me and replenish my light. Relationship taught me to approach the Throne for myself, and that I had a direct line of communication to God.

Religion taught me that I had to be timid a meek. Relationship taught me to be radical and relentless in my pursuit of God. Religion taught me to sit and wait on God to act. Relationship taught me that Faith Without Works is DEAD!

Relationship taught me that I was equipped with

EVERYTHING that I needed to gain wealth. Relationship taught me that wealth wasn't merely paper currency. It was me realizing who I was, and Whose I was!

For years, a wounded spirit would hinder me from approaching the Throne of God for myself because I felt I was unworthy. I can't count how many times that someone has called me for prayer. They thought that I had some kind of special connection or workaround to God. I am happy to tell them that God can speak to them just as He speaks to me. All it takes is a RELATIONSHIP.

Relationships are hard work. I can't speak for anyone else, but I know I had issues with being consistent. I didn't want to surrender. I wasn't going to allow anyone or anything to retake my power. I wanted to be in control. The desire to always be in control would only send me spiraling out of control. I would repeat these actions because I didn't slow down to repair them. I also didn't know how, or have the tools even to attempt to correct them.

Religion taught me that I needed a title and had to be perfect to move forward. Relationship taught me I just needed to move. Some days I could walk a mile, and other days I would limp. I would get up, draw back the curtains, invite the light in, and muster up a smile.

They Gave Me Religion, Be Not Conformed

I wake up Sunday morning

And put on my shoes
Put my tithes in my purse
I've got to pay my dues
They didn't teach me tithes were also
My talents and time
They only stressed that it was only a dime
A tenth of my earnings
Relationship taught me
 It's His money, not mine
Relationship taught me
 I was His currency
But before I....
I walked about smiling
All the while confused
You see
I know who God is
They taught me that
I know what His commandments say
They gave me a tract
I know when the song comes on to wave my hand
I know to show I'm grateful
In the form of a dance
I know what they fed me
Because daily I eat
I know to pray before I sleep
 wake and eat
I know to pause before I enter the doors
When they are praying in the sanctuary
I know love conquers all
Yet sometimes our actions are contrary
Excuse me if I am out of line
Charge it to my heart and not my mind

This is what baffles me
We should be set apart
But not absent in the streets
The world needs His heart
We need to show the world
That greater is He that resides in me
And it's only because
I kneel at His feet
We make it look easy
We forget to let them know
We serve a real and true God
It's not a show
We need to remind them
We were not always saved
And we are only alive because of His grace
I know what religion is within these walls
But I can't make sense of it
or how it pertains to the call
When I was young
We fed the poor
We gave people hugs when they walked
through those doors
We didn't ask questions
It left me wanting more
I wanted more than rules and dramatic quotes
I wanted more than emotions
Crafted by highs and lows
I wanted less judgment and laughter
When they didn't hit the right notes
The word reminds us to make a joyful noise
Yet we won't allow people to serve
If they don't hit the right cord

We turn a blind eye to pack the pews
We use people for their giftings
When they make mistakes
We throw them away like refuse
We sell concerts and tickets
Instead of sharing the good news
We speak of love
in the same breath
Cut people down with abuse
We speak Gods word mixed with our own
 out the side of our face
When our words part our lips
God is not pleased with the taste
When will we lose religion
And chase relationship with all of our might
In the end
Will you hear well done faithful servant
You fought the good fight?
Please don't take offense
I want revelation and insight
To my Father's Heart
But religion and titles
Drive us apart
Don't get me wrong I give reverence where due
But what good are titles
If people can't approach you
We've gotten so big were so far removed
Yet Jesus was with the people
He ate the word
He taught the word
He applied the word
He was the word

He served
He broke bread with King
Court and criminals
He didn't need grand entrances
He was humble and nimble
He could change your life
In the blink of the eye
Because of His grace and the love inside

I went far too many years in search of the perfect relationship, and finally, I would learn the key to the ideal relationship was there all along. I would now have my eyes opened to see what God was showing me. I didn't feel compelled to look to man for what God could tell me. I would now be able to serve in church past the cycles of church hurt.

My language would be that of love. I now would understand the importance of speaking life over myself, and family while correcting myself and others in love. If it did not edify, I would be mindful not to say it. I would vow to leave others better than I found them. I would now be able to pray for those that persecuted me. I would ask God daily to show me how to deal with His people.

I would now understand that God loved the sinner and the saint, and nothing we could do would change that. I asked God to break my heart for what broke His, and for the first time in my life, I felt of value. He gave me a glimpse of my future, and He gave me life. When people betrayed me, He would have me try to understand why they did the things that they did.

I would be a continual work in process; however, He would not allow me to use that as a crutch to lash out and hurt others. He gave me a heart for His people. I am in no way attempting to persuade you that I am now a saint. What I need you to know is that I am now aware. I would no longer allow people to project their deficiencies and issues on me. I would soon understand that backbiting was a form of witchcraft, and I would be mindful of the words that I spoke over people.

I would understand that the issues that I disliked about others in some way shape or form, resided in me and I would need to address those issues. I would try each day to be better than the person I was the day before. I'd strive to have people feel my love instead of my empty words.

I began to understand that every trial and tribulation that I faced in life was necessary for what God had planned for my life. The word reminds us to whom much is given, much is required, Luke 12:48.

I would not take my life's challenges for granted, they now were viewed as purposeful by design, and I was the Master's piece. I would also try to be the Master's Peace! Jesus had suffered mightily for me, and I would try my best not to disappoint Him.

God had saved me from myself, no one else held power to destroy me. That gave me a freedom that is inexplicable. I no longer felt obligated to carry the sins of anyone else. The sharp pangs of insults no longer penetrated my heart like they use to. I would forgive and move on. I, and like others before me would realize that hurt people hurt people, but healed people would work together to heal others.

It's surprising that I could now see the correlation between pain and purpose, and that you could not have one without the other! I would be one of the blessed ones who learned that before my sunset.

I'm sorry, but I refuse to live up
to your expectations of me
I can no longer look through
the lenses you crafted for me
I can no longer pulse my heart to beat at your rate
I can no longer accept the love that is really hate
You hate the fact that I'm me
You hate the fact that you can't mold me
to be a mirror you
I choose to overlook the things you do
The things you say
The way you manipulate me to respond a certain way
You see you don't see my value
You keep shooting arrows
Those fiery darts trying to pierce my heart
See you're pretty smart
But I'm smarter
I was built to go farther
And you're just a mile up the road

You can't carry the load
That I'm carrying
These feelings that I've been burying
are trying to surface
But you don't deserve this
This being my time
Studying the lines, you're trying to feed me
See I'm not hungry
And your soul is empty
You try to belittle me
While pretending, you're helping
All the while seeking to devour me
The news you see is
That I have power
Even if it's down to the 11th hour
He will rescue me

I was hungry for more! I wanted more answers. I wanted more time! Like the great Maxine Waters, I was reclaiming my time! I found out an essential ingredient to the sauce. I learned that everything around us can be falling apart, and we can still be of use to God. We don't have to be perfect, we just have to be available. We have to be willing, and we have to be naked before the world.

That's the problem with a lot of us, if I can speak freely. We are accustomed to wearing masks and not being vulnerable. We hide behind makeup and work, we hide behind money and name brands. We are afraid to be found out, and that is exhausting! I was that person. I felt if I were successful, it would cover up all of my flaws and people would love me.

The thing about success, strength, and new levels is that with each new level you will encounter new devils. New battles and new lessons. The enemy will always attempt to replicate what God produces. In these moments in life, a relationship with God is a must.

You must trust God's direction and accept His correction, as it is ultimately for your good. One must rely on discernment, and that comes from spending time with God to clearly hear what He is articulating. Discernment is a must! You will receive different opportunities, and you must have the ability to know which table to eat from, and what cup to drink from in order not to get poisoned.

Remember we talked earlier about soul ties, the ties that bind, and those that attempt to tether to your destiny. I learned the hard way that every connection wasn't a good connection. I began to look for God Connections. If God wasn't in it, neither was I. I had experienced too much hurt to go backward. The problem is, I still held a soft heart, and that at times made me a target of predators.

Eventually, I would learn the gift of goodbye via bumps, bruises and sleepless nights. Better late than never is the phrase that surfaces, as it pertains to the gift of goodbye. Goodbye doesn't mean that you no longer love the thing or person that you are leaving, it just means that you understand that it no longer serves a purpose in your life.

God finally saw fit to repair those broken places in my life. There was a song by Tasha Cobbs that explained it all for me, that song would be called "Gracefully Broken." God had been gracefully breaking me for His use for decades, and I would finally submit and move in the direction He wanted me to go, and our relationship would be fantastic.

I began to see the beauty inside of myself. I could be alone and love my presence. The fact that I would start to be okay being alone with my thoughts was a feat in itself! That is the accurate measure of wholeness, if you can stand being alone with your thoughts and not want to run, you have grown tremendously.

Silence is uncomfortable; however, it is in the absence of sound that you will indeed begin to hear with clarity. I found out a lot about myself in the quiet season of my life. It was a challenging period for me. It was in this season, that God would reveal that I had been tethered to a sexual demon. I had carried that demon for nearly 40 years.

The only time that I would be vulnerable to the enemy's tricks was when I was at rest. I was spending the night with one of my divine connections, and my sister from another mister Robin Sanders. We had planned the next morning at Praise Tabernacle in Sunrise, and it was time for bed.

I felt a little anxious that night, and I couldn't explain it. I would fall asleep listening to the Word, that was the only way that I could keep my mind occupied and away from the reoccurring nightmares which would attempt to pull me back into the darkness. The enemy will do anything to remind us of our past and try to prevent us from walking into our future, it had an habit of attacking me in my dreams.

That night I would toss and turn, and I would be restless. I would feel aroused in my sleep, and I felt a familiar feeling coming over me. There was a beautiful, mysterious figure, and I could not make out who it was. As it got closer, I tried to retreat, and it latched on to me and would not let go. I couldn't explain it. The more I tried to pull away from it, the tighter it held onto me. And then it happened, God removed the veil, and I saw my sexual demon.

I was in a fight for my life, it wanted me back, and I refused to go back. The face alone was enough to paralyze the strongest of saints. The face was gnarled, and it didn't want to let me go. I fought and fought, and finally, I woke up crying. I was so upset, and I was planning to hold it in, but holding it in would do me no good. If I learned anything I knew I couldn't fight it alone. I had to confront it. This time I had an ally. I had God, and I had a prayer warrior.

I was no longer ashamed. I called Robin into the room, explained what happened, and she said six words that helped change the game. All she said was, "Now we know how to pray!" We would pray and keep it moving.

She never judged, she never brought it up again, and she would love me into submission.

CHAPTER 8

Healed and Still Healing

I AM GRATEFUL FOR ALL OF THE CHALLENGES THAT LIFE allowed to shape me, as a result of those challenges, I have grown spiritually, emotionally and physically and I have been healed in many areas of my life and in others I am still healing.

It is important for me to share the life lessons that I've been taught, that have brought me to the place that I am at today. I haven't arrived and I probably wont ever get to the place where I can say that I have. In life we should strive to be lifelong learners. We should continue to assess ourselves often and do mirror checks daily.

It takes a conscious decision to love people in spite of. It is extremely easy to love others when life is good and people are on their best behavior. This is probably one reason that there are so many broken marriages and families today. I have two broken marriages. I placed unrealistic expectations on others and expected them to love like I did.

One thing that I have learned is that I can't expect people to love like I do because they haven't faced the challenges that I did. I am going to ask you to stop whatever you are doing at this moment and gauge the temperature of your heart. There are no right or wrong answers to these questions, the goal is for you to reflect and be open to adjusting your perspective if you don't like what you see.

HEART TEMPERATURE CHECK

Ask yourself the following questions:

- Do I place unrealistic expectation on those around me and hold them accountable for disappointment?
- Do I take more than I am willing to give?
- Do others have to ask for help or do I see a need and volunteer?
- Do I sow into the business of my family and friends?
- When looking for volunteer activities, do you first ask what's in it for me?
- What is my first response when someone brings a problem to me that I have the resources to assist?
- Am I willing to share my resources with others without want of anything in return?
- Do I hold grudges, but expect others to freely forgive

me?

- Do I share knowledge when I gain it or do I keep it for myself?

Did your answers surprise you? I know that as simple as those questions appear, they make you really think about the posture or temperature of your heart. Again daily, I make it a point to assess my heart to ensure that I am walking the talk. When I leave this earth, I want the legacy that I leave to be one of love. I want people to understand that their current situation doesn't not reflect their future.

If you were honest with yourself you now have a glimpse of what you need to work on and more important-ly, now you can address those character flaws and move on. Life's experiences have a way of making you self-reflect often when you become aware of who you are and aspire to be. The day I entered that mental institution was the wakeup call that I so desperately needed.

Looking back on my life, I can't believe that I am alive today. With everything that I carried, I should have been dead a long time ago, but God I am alive and now my mission would be to help everyone that I can realize that they have potential and that they can achieve any-thing if they shift their mindset to see the positive in every challenging situation. I didn't know what I wanted to do to help people, but I knew I had to do something. Truth be told the only real skill-set I had was love for others. I was able to feel their pain and influence them to change or at least consider it.

MANOS, ESPERANZA Y HUMANIDAD. EL MISIONERO (HANDS, HOPE, AND HUMANITY. THE MISSIONARY)

In 2014, I was blessed with the opportunity to go on a mission trip to Cartagena, Colombia I asked no questions or had any real reservations, all I knew was that there was something pulling me and there had to be more that I could do and I wanted to try. I remember the day I arrived in Colombia the air was very different. I reminded me of safety.

I can't explain why it felt like safety but it did. I was in a foreign land, I did not speak the language, but I was determined to make an impact. If you haven't figured it by now I have a heart as soft as butter and I willingly share the pain of others. Cartagena changed my life and taught me a very valuable lesson. The people had so little as it pertained to things of monetary value, yet they were rich in culture, and they were rich in love.

I went there thinking I was going to serve and my life was forever changed. It was so liberating seeing people who had nothing and lived in what we would consider a shed in the US be so free, so giving and so loving. I mean their situation based on man's standard would leave one depressed. I remember one day we were at one of the schools we were renovating and I was tired so I decided to take a break.

I love to doodle. It takes my mind off of things. So I began to doodle like always and I feel a tap on my shoulder and I hear permiso, I look up and this little brown face is smiling at me so I motion for one of our team members to come over and translate. They go back and forth for a minute and the child wanted to know my name and why I didn't speak Spanish.

They didn't understand why my skin looked like theirs and we couldn't communicate. I attempted to let them know I was American, soy Americana and that I lived in Florida. Soy viven en Florida. Look please don't expect me to be perfect, laughing out loud but I tried. These kids deserved a medal they were very kind and patient with me. Well anyhow as I sat there struggling, and that is an understatement through this conversation, I asked one of the four if they wanted me to draw them a picture.

It was nothing fancy, I doodled their name on a piece of napkin and gave them a crayon and then the other three requested the same. I grabbed a couple of napkins and proceeded to draw their names in various bubble scripts and design never really looking up but to hand them their names and send them on their way. I didn't notice that a line was beginning to form and was bending the corner. As soon as I would finish doodling for one they would run and get another child.

I can't remember who it was, but all the sudden I felt a tap on my shoulder and they asked me to look up. I looked up and there had to be at least twenty kids in line waiting for me to doodle their name on a piece of paper so they could color it! Can you imagine that. Some of our kids are so spoiled here in the states. They have every kind of technology in the world and yet the have the audacity to claim boredom.

We stand in line for hours at a time for a concert ticket, a video game or a movie, and here they were ecstatic to get a small paper napkin with their name scribbled on it. I was in awe! Well I finished that task and I was taken on a small tour in the community. I visited many homes and was opened up to the brutal reality of true poverty.

I saw babies that were encouraged to have babies to assist with bringing an extra ten dollars a month into the home as a benefit from the government. Ten WHOLE DOLLARS! I would later learn that the average income was 200 dollars per month and the cost of living was 260! Each home I would visit my heart would break a little more. By the time we had finished our rounds I had given all of my money away and had tear stained eyes. Man, my heart ached!

One of the things that stuck out in my mind the most, actually there were two, the first was meeting the grandmother that had to take care of all of her grandchildren because her daughter, the children's mother was electrocuted by faulty wiring in the home. She cried in my arms as I embraced her and my heart was numb.

The second incident that took my breath away was meeting the family where both parents and grandparents were present in the home as well as all of the children. They had makeshift furniture a dirt floor, their kitchen was on the outside, which pretty much consisted of wood hammer together to place a kettle type pot on, yet again they were joyful and they stuck together.

As we left each household we offered to pray and they graciously accepted it. There was a baby with no clothes or diaper on and she was crying I asked for permission to hold her, she was so beautiful. I can still remember her abuela watching me hold the baby, which would be the last time I would hold her. She died months after from diarrhea. Her family could not afford the money to take her to the doctor or get her medicine.

I would return to serve the following year and I would leave full and exhausted. I would pour out everything I possibly could to try and bring hope to some one else. The more I served the better I felt. I t actually made me stronger, I felt empowered, I felt whole. The third year would find me in Honduras. Again serving. Again, pouring out my light into others again loving and growing mentally. Physically and spiritually. Every chance I would get to serve and share my story to uplift someone else I would feel invincible. I would no longer feel the shame that was my life.

I learned that everything, every painful moment in my life served a purpose it was shaping me to walk in my calling. I didn't not realize that all of the years that I spent away from my family God would be building me. I didn't realize that God would turn my trauma into a testimony that would one day help someone else be liberated.

I didn't realize that with each speaking engagement God was building my influence and opening doors while simultaneously preparing to close others. Each step took me higher on my journey to the summit and then finally one day I would reach the mount of the summit and God would push me and grant me wings on the way down. He knew I was an eagle and He had granted me my wings.

God Gave Me Wings

Today you gave me wings
I didn't know I could fly
Before I wouldn't attempt to try
I didn't know I had power
Every hour I thought of a reason to give up
And then I drank from your cup
You had the magic potion
Instilled in me the notion
That I mattered
Life was scattered
With thunderstorms
Pure reign
Cloudy with a chance
Of Greatness
You blessed this
Mess
Age with grace

CHAPTER 8: HEALED AND STILL HEALING

I found my place in you
My faith in you
You paid my dues
And coined me
The Master's peace

For years I was given opportunities that a person from my upbringing should never have had the chance to experience. I sat at tables with CEO's, founders, small business owners, women and men in leadership and I stood out. I was different in a good way and I would continue to be granted favor. I was afforded the opportunity to speak as a panelist for the National Coalition of 100 Black Women, at Barry University on the Social Change Model, I served as an Event Chair and moderator for the National Diversity Council.

The list could go on and on about God's unmerited favor and grace that was extended to me, but for the sake of time I will refrain. I will just have to get it in during our personal time together. Sometimes I sit in awe and quiet trying to figure out why God heart was soft for me. He loved me when I didn't love myself and He was patient and a true gentleman about it.

I recall the time that my granddaddy Mack would sit down on the sofa in front of me, grandma Madea called it the settee, and in a low but strong voice He would say four words that would cause me to often self-reflect. He said God is watching you. God was watching me; my granddaddy was a very wise man. I thought of him as the gentle giant. He knew there was something inside of me and I didn't.

Recalling that statement is one of the very reasons I thought it relevant to assist others with understanding and uncovering their potential. I must admit I became obsessed with the idea of seeing people win. I would push people and I would tell my story, at first it was very uncomfortable being vulnerable to others

I began to understand the power in getting naked before God and man. Its quite ironic that being naked before man initially would birth dysfunction and later in life it would liberate me. I think about how I was unwilling to have my flaws on display and now I don't even bat an eye. I said it before and I will say it again, God has a sense of humor and uses it often when teaching us lessons.

Na·ked: (of a person or part of the body) without clothes ("he'd never seen a naked woman before."); (of something such as feelings or behavior) undisguised; blatant ("naked, unprovoked aggression.")

Synonyms: undisguised, plain, unadorned, unvarnished, unqualified, stark, bald

Naked Before You

Allow me to be naked before
Undressed before you
Tested by you
Vested by you
Moved by you
Used by you
Renewed by you
Improved by you
Tried through the fire
And branded by you
Abandoned at youth
Yet now I am fireproof
I can stand in battle
Because I am covered by you
I can walk the journey
I have endurance in you
Beauty in you
Peace in you
Wisdom in you
Speak the truth through you
No more leaks in you
I found love in you
I wait in you
No more waste in you

There was a renewal of my mind, a shift of sorts from the person dysfunction attempted to mold me to be and towards what purpose designed me to be. The word reminds us that timing is everything. In this season of my life it would be a time to pluck, heal, build up, a time to embrace, gather, love and speak. The caged bird was caged no more.

Grace gave me a voice and all of the necessary tools to begin my journey. It is said where God gives you a vision He will also provide the provision. He set people, places and things before me to accomplish the tasks He set before. It didn't matter all the years I ran, what was important was the day that I would finally surrender. I would trust Him with my whole heart and I would move.

In 2012 Heal the City Campaign was birth from decades of pain, tears, trials and adversity.

The mission of the Heal the city conference is to bring together a dynamic group of leaders that will uplift, motivate, and inspire individuals to live their best life now, no matter the challenges they face. The panelist through thought-provoking discussions will reveal how they overcame obstacles that are seldom discussed that plague our society as a whole. Topics will include mental health, molestation, domestic abuse, sexual health and well-being, leadership, and spiritual health. The goal is to provide sustainable, valuable resources to heal our families, individuals, and cities, in a safe and non-judgmental environment. It was important for me to have people understand that they were not an afterthought and that they were purposed by design.

Even though I began the campaign in 2012 it would not be until 2018 that I would incorporate Heal the City as an official entity. The catalyst for that change would happen January the 25th of 2018 when I received a phone call out of the blue letting me know that I no longer had a position due to restructuring in the organization, that's another story all together.

It was a strange feeling, I had at the time no savings in the bank and no desire to leave the organization. That's where the sense of humor of a great and mighty God comes in. Truth be told, I had been speaking for years how there had to be more and that my current view couldn't possibly be all that God had to offer for me.

When I hung up the phone from that conversation such a peace fell over me as if God was saying every time you got promoted you thought I was giving you the best. Now I am going to show you a glimpse of what I am about to walk you into. I was in awe then and I am still in awe. That phone call left me un-bothered and unafraid.

I had surgery the past December and God sustained me for weeks without pay and I lacked nothing. There was nothing broken, nothing lacking and nothing missing! In fact, in this season I gave more with less than I ever gave with a steady income. Between the period of January and April 90,000 US dollars have funneled its way into my bank account and out in the way of businesses, a tee shirt line, a jewelry line and other business ventures.

I was now an entrepreneur and while God was teaching me how to use everything He equipped me with to gain wealth, He would use me as a model to teach others. He gave me a work ethic that wouldn't quit. He mended my heart and increased my joy. He made my walk look incredibly easy, even though it was far from that.

There were many nights that I was at the brink of a meltdown, this time however I had an army of prayer warriors and I had developed through relationship my own powerful prayer life. The Inaugural Heal the City would take place in Homestead Florida, it was an amazing event and the community, which was 98% Latino really came together for it. Only about thirty people registered for the event and I felt like a failure. Then as they trickled in over 125 people were involved in the event. My heart melted.

I would go into the next event the following year in the city of Fort Lauderdale at the African American Cultural Library and Research Center. I was super excited I had well over 200 people registered for the event. Event day came and only about 30 people showed including the speakers. It hurt me that my community of peers did not want healing. It was a free event and I poured my heart soul and tears into the community.

God taught me a very valuable lesson that year. He taught me it wasn't about numbers It was about impact and being faithful in the little things. I couldn't understand why as a race we would be quick to buy concert tickets to the latest up and coming recording artist but we couldn't invest in ourselves for FREE.

I would continue to bring the movement to city after city pouring out and then it began building a momentum. People wanted transparency and authentic leadership. They wanted to get unstuck and to find a way out. I was more than glad to assist by granting real life, eating, breathing, soft hearted and gracefully broken others like myself to take the platform and find freedom!

I wasn't concerned about big names as they draw groupies. I needed unknown people who had been through some things, who had nothing to lose. I wanted to have people whose hearts broke for what broke God's. If you have never walked through what I have walked through I can't relate to you. And that's What Heal the City offered people. Heal the City brought transformational leadership to the broken, the dysfunctional, the functioning hurt and it gave them an outlet and resources to heal.

Each event brought new challenges and new divine connections. Each time Heal the City entered new community we upped the ante. We moved faster and dug deeper. We poured our lives into others and the benefits always outweighed the challenges. I could see an army of equipped individuals being woven together to spread healing, love and awareness across the earth and God would allow me to lead the charge.

As I look back over my life I would not change one experience, the only thing that I can say I wish that I had awakened from my slumber much earlier. I feel that I wasted so much time and could have cause less hurt than I did. I was wounding when I should have been healing and helping. Had I awakened earlier I could have saved my children from experiencing so much grief.

I could have made better relationship choices that would have had more of a positive impact on my children. I would have prayed harder and I would have spent more time building a relationship with God. I would have been able to weave biblical principals in to my family's DNA. We live and we learn. We lose and hopefully we make better choices.

I count it a blessing to wake up each day and get to see my beautiful children. I have had many sleepless nights as it pertained to them, yet I am aware that we all have our struggles and have a journey to take. I know that I cannot carry their burdens for them and at times wish I could. I know they have to make their own paths, make their own mistakes and gain wisdom via life's lessons.

The goal for my children is to ensure they are equipped to handle the pressures that this life may throw at them. To avoid the predators and for God to spare their lives. I have prayed that specific prayer on multiple occasions. I pray that they find they are worthy of love and find families where that love can be reciprocated.

We all wander this earth longing to find our perfect fit. I am not even sure if there is such a thing as a perfect anything. Sometimes the more we receive the more we want. In this time in my life I want more of God, more of relationship and like many more authenticity and transparency. I want to be surrounded by whole people who are willing to risk it all to assist others heal.

We all fight battles and have scars. My wish is that before we open our mouths our hearts will remind us that we all are more alike than we are different and that we are stronger together than we are apart. A house divided cannot stand. I probably mentioned it before but Henry B Fernandez stated that if you want to destroy America destroy the family, there were no truer words.

Dr. Myles Monroe pointed out that the richest place on the earth is, was, and will be the graveyard. That statement alone would change how I viewed life and how I would approach each new challenge going forward. My overarching goal would be to leave this life and shell of a body empty. I would pour out every gift I had into others. I would leave each individual that I came in contact with better than I found them and I would love without limits.

I would lead every horse I could find to water and I would love them into submission until they drank from the well. I would focus on the dehydrated and spiritually anemic and remind them that iron sharpens iron and I would stand in the trenches with them armed for battle.

Every chance I would get I would project my peace on others. I would allow love to be my weapon of choice and I would win time and time again. If someone spoke against I would not attempt to vindicate myself because I now understood that my energy, time and efforts would have to be used wisely.

I would remember to stay away from battles and wars that did not lend to receiving spoils. I would understand that not every argument required my attention and I would be better for that in the end. I would finally be whole, healed and usable. I would work towards the goal of healing the world one city at a time, starting with me. *She Blinked!*

About **The Author**

Laurinda Andujar, a Florida native and mother of three, coins herself a survivor due to overcoming a challenging childhood. In a desperate search for hope and an outlet for the things that she held secret. She would ultimately find solace in writing and poetry. These healing tools along with a relationship with God would quickly become a means of escape for her.

Laurinda has earned many certifications in public speaking and attended the School of the Prophets in Fort Lauderdale Florida at the Henry B. Fernandez Institute of Biblical Studies. The National Diversity Council has recognized her, as well as the National Coalition of 100 Black Women, Barry University and other organizations for service. She has spoken both domestically and internationally to assist others with healing using the transformational leadership methodology.

After leaving her organization of nearly 27 years Laurinda Founded Heal the City Inc and SheBlinked LLC, both are public speaking organizations, that aim to assist individuals with recognizing their purpose in life. Laurinda wholeheartedly believes that a person's situation can be broken and that they still can walk out their God-given mission, being a survivor of molestation, domestic violence, suicide attempts, and grief, she aims to use her positivity and light to heal the world one city at a time. Laurinda is currently working towards obtaining a certification in grief counseling.

To contact author, go to:

www.SheBlinked.com
www.HealTheCityInc.org
sheblinked314@gmail.com
Instagram: heal_the_city_inc.
Facebook: Laurinda Andujar